Whom Does The Constitution Command?

Recent Titles in
Contributions in Legal Studies
Series Editor: Paul L. Murphy

Whom Does The Constitution Command?

A CONCEPTUAL ANALYSIS WITH PRACTICAL IMPLICATIONS

Larry Alexander
&
Paul Horton

CONTRIBUTIONS IN LEGAL STUDIES, NUMBER 42

Greenwood Press

New York • Westport, Connecticut • London

Library of Congress Cataloging-in-Publication Data

Alexander, Lawrence A.
  Whom does the Constitution command? : a conceptual analysis with
practical implications / Larry Alexander and Paul Horton.
    p. cm. — (Contributions in legal studies, ISSN 0147-1074 ;
no. 42)
  Includes bibliographies and index.
  ISBN 0-313-26216-0 (lib. bdg. : alk. paper)
    1. United States—Constitutional law. 2. State action—United
States. 3. Constitutional torts—United States. I. Horton, Paul.
II. Title. III. Series.
KF4550.A729 1988
342.73—dc19
[347.302]   87-32272

British Library Cataloguing in Publication Data is available.

Library of Congress Catalog Card Number: 87-32272
ISBN: 0-313-26216-0
ISSN: 0147-1074

First published in 1988

Greenwood Press, Inc.
88 Post Road West, Westport, Connecticut 06881

Printed in the United States of America

The paper used in this book complies with the
Permanent Paper Standard issued by the National
Information Standards Organization (Z39.48-1984).

10 9 8 7 6 5 4 3 2 1

We dedicate our first book to Elaine Alexander and Jacklyn Horton, whom we admire for, among countless other things, their extraordinary tolerance, perseverance, and skills as lawyers.

Contents

Diagrams

Preface

In a way, our book is about some of the most intractable yet well-known doctrines of U.S. constitutional law: "state action," "under color of law," and their near relatives. We examine these doctrines in light of a root question, a question that is posed nearly every time the doctrines come into play but that is almost never articulated or answered in anything like a comprehensible way.

The root question, of course, is this: who are the bearers of the various duties imposed by the U.S. Constitution? In other words, whom does the Constitution command? This is the question that doctrinal monsters like "state action" and "under color of law" are designed, more subconsciously than consciously, to answer.

In our examination of this root question, we develop and explain several possible models that might serve to provide its answer. Although our purposes here are primarily exegetical in character—there is today surprisingly large room for straightforward exegesis—we conclude that only two of the possible models (we call them the "Legalist" and the "Naturalist") are fully principled. And, in the course of our examination, we reach some other conclusions as well.

First, if "state action" (including its doctrinal near relatives) turns out to be a disguised stand-in for certain substantive constitutional values, then the concept is ill suited for such a task. Employment of the doctrine to such an end results, predictably, in Supreme Court decisions that are internally inconsistent and, on occasion, patently unjustifiable applications of the underlying substantive values.

Second, if "state action" (including its doctrinal near relatives) refers to the conceptual issue of who are the bearers of constitutional duties, then the concept does not affect the substantive merits of lawsuits. Rather, it affects only the question of whether a lawsuit may be prosecuted in federal court as well as in state court (and perhaps also who the defendant to the lawsuit should be).

Two appendices are included in this book. Each has freestanding vitality. In the first, we set forth a chronological catalogue of the major post-Civil War Supreme Court cases that deal obviously with the "state action" issues, and comment briefly on them in light of the models described in the text. In the second, we deal with the application of our models to "constitutional torts," an area of great current interest that seems especially in need of cogent resolution of the issue of whom the Constitution commands.

Undeniably, our efforts have received immeasurable aid from those who have toiled in this vineyard before us. We gratefully acknowledge the extremely valuable comments and criticisms of earlier manuscript versions of this book, bestowed upon us by Carl Auerbach, Paul Brest, Erwin Chemerinsky, Michael Perry, Maimon Schwarzschild, and Chris Wonnell. Whatever the quality of this our final product, it has been significantly improved by their contributions. Collegiality can have no finer expression than their assistance. We also are deeply grateful for Amy Powell's diligent research for, and Roanne Shamsky's excellent typing and retyping of the several stages of, this effort.

1

Introduction

Within the legal system of the United States, the Constitution's dictates reign supreme wherever they are conceded to reach. But, to what extent does the Constitution reach within the legal system of the United States? Where, at any given point in time, and if at all, does "constitutional law" leave off and "plain old law" remain to occupy the rest of the U.S. legal system's field of play?

New arrivals to these questions would have warrant to suppose that, after 200 years of constitutional reign, their answers would have been deduced with at least theoretical if not scientifically practical completeness and precision. After casual acquaintance with these questions, however, novitiates will discover that, especially with respect to some of the Constitution's most important provisions, they still remain to be answered in an authoritative way.

Suppose the relatively simple instance in which a citizen is alleged to have infringed the entitlement of government or of another citizen. The entitlement, and the manner by which it may be infringed, may have been defined in a state or federal statute, or it may have been defined by resort to the common law. Redress of the infringement is pursued in a criminal or civil action. In defense the infringer, stipulating that she infringed the alleged entitlement, claims that the law that defines the entitlement is unconstitutional. If the law is declared to be not unconstitutional, then has the infringer simply violated the law, or has she violated the Constitution as well?

Although the answer to this question—and to many related questions that arise from many related instances—has not been settled with authority, the need for an answer would seem to be a desperate one. Whole areas of litigation, especially in the federal courts, continue to beg for theoretical rationale and resolution mainly because questions like this one have not been answered with authority. In particular, the large and amorphous domains of "state action," actions "under color of law," and "federal judicial abstention" suffer by virtue of failure to achieve a definitive answer to these sorts of questions.

The answer to the question of where "constitutional law" leaves off and "plain old law" begins independently of "constitutional law" cannot be given until another question is raised and answered: whom does the Constitution command? Put differently: does the Constitution speak to and impose legal obligations upon a limited class of governmental institutions (and their human members); or does it speak to and impose legal obligations upon a broader class, such as the class of "all citizens"?

This is the question we explicate in this book. In the explication, we will explore the three main possible answers to the question of whom the Constitution commands—and three other possible answers—as suggested in the case law of the Supreme Court of the United States. We introduce the contours of the question we raise, the importance of achieving an authoritative answer to it, and the project of our book, as follows:

Let us imagine an ideal state of affairs from the standpoint of the Constitution. Suppose some value is enshrined in the Constitution. This constitutional value—CV, whatever it may be—may mandate that some law or set of laws be enacted and enforced, may prohibit some laws from being enacted and enforced, or may do both of these things.[1]

Within its ambit, CV will be realized to the maximum extent possible if the following conditions obtain:

1. The relevant government has enacted a set of laws that CV prescribes for its realization (and has refrained from enacting laws that CV prohibits). This set of laws will include duty-imposing laws, remedial laws (in the event the duty-imposing laws are breached), and procedural laws (to effectuate remedies in the event of breach).

2. The relevant government has enacted laws that CV prescribes for the selection, training, and governance of the officials who will administer the set of duty-imposing, remedial, and procedural laws. In addition, the relevant government has enacted laws that CV prescribes for the appropriate allocation of resources for the enforcement of these other laws.

3. The relevant officials are in fact obeying all laws prescribed by CV.

4. All citizens subject to the duty-imposing laws imposed by CV are in fact obeying those laws.

In such an ideal state of affairs—ideal, at least, for *CV*—*CV* would be so completely realized that no claims within its ambit would ever arise.

We must pause here to eliminate a possible implication or two that might have been taken from the picture we have drawn of the ideal state of affairs for *CV*.

First, we reaffirm the view, shared by nearly everyone, that no constitutional value properly can be idealized in a vacuum. We enthusiastically concede that the Constitution contemplates a number of values, that the values thus contemplated come into conflict with each other at innumerable points on a more or less continual basis, and that giving the "vacuum" treatment to any particular constitutional value cannot furnish the last word of any serious inquiry into the appropriate ambit and strength of that value.

If, however, there were a single constitutional value (or if a single constitutional value could be constructed in amalgam form—a sentence as long as a book, perhaps—from all constitutional values taken together), *then* the conditions we have described above would comprise the ideal state of affairs for that constitutional value. And this hypothetically ideal description is all we need for the point we intend here.[2]

Second—an observation that may well follow from the first—realization of *CV* "to the maximum possible extent" does not entail the notion that only one particular set of laws must be enacted and administered in one particular manner. The conditions we have identified for maximization of *CV* are complex ones, even when those conditions are set forth in a vacuum. Variations between relevant governments with respect to one condition (for example, in remedial laws) may well be counterbalanced by other variations with respect to other conditions (for example, in resource-allocation laws).

We are prepared to concede that, within the constraints imposed by the Constitution, it is conceivable that *CV* may be realized to its maximum possible extent by an indefinite variety of sets of duty-imposing, remedial, procedural, official-selection-and-training, and resource-allocation laws, their administration, and methodologies of obedience to them. The point, then, is that our project in this book is indifferent to these matters, to arguments over whether any particular set of these laws is required to maximize *CV*.

Bogus implications aside, appropriate implications remain. The conditions we have identified for maximal realization of *CV* suggest various possible pathologies, the presence of which will portend less than maximal realization of *CV*. The following pathologies come immediately to mind:

1. Citizens might disobey the duty-imposing laws prescribed by *CV*, requiring in response the invocation of *CV*-prescribed remedial and

procedural laws and other components of the relevant government's administrative apparatus.

2. Officials of the relevant government might transgress the duty-imposing laws prescribed by CV—perhaps by refusing to follow the laws requiring them to enforce other laws prescribed by CV—mandating in response the enforcement by other officials of still other laws prescribed by CV for dealing with miscreant officials.

3. The relevant government's lawmakers may fail to enact some or all of the various laws—duty-imposing, remedial, procedural, administrative, resource-allocative, and so forth—that are prescribed by CV, with the result that the government's relevant set of laws, taken in its entirety, is inappropriate to maximize CV. Or the relevant government's lawmakers may enact a law that is prohibited by CV, with the same result.

These, we think, are the main pathologies that, if they occur, would result in a failure to maximize CV.

The stipulation comfortably is in order that each of the pathologies offending constitutional values entails a violation of law, whether by citizen, by official, or by government. The question then becomes: Of the pathologies offending a constitutional value that we have identified, which pathology or pathologies represent an *unconstitutional* state of affairs?

Put differently, which of these pathologies amount to *constitutional violations*, as opposed merely to violations of law? Put still differently: Does it make good sense, for worthwhile purposes, to distinguish among these various pathologies by calling some of them "unconstitutional pathologies" and others "nonconstitutional pathologies"?

One possibly worthwhile purpose for making distinctions may be brought to mind by embellishing upon our stipulation, as follows: Not only does each of these pathologies entail a violation of law, but also each entails a violation of law for which some court is available to mete out some form of redress. *Some* court; but *which* court? And thus the inquiry is suggested: How are we to deal with these pathologies within that portion of our federal system that is composed of federal courts and state courts?

The inquiry suggested here, which invites an approach to our larger project from a narrow but very important perspective, gives us a glimpse of part of the stakes that may be involved in the answering of our broader question. The problem that comes into view, of course, is that (1) currently state courts are many while federal courts are few; (2) currently the great bulk of litigation in our country is handled in our state courts; (3) the subject matter jurisdiction of the federal courts overlaps significantly the more expansive subject matter jurisdiction of the state courts; (4) although the federal courts have only limited subject matter jurisdiction with respect to claims of nonconstitutional violations of law, they have practically unlimited jurisdiction with respect to claims of constitutional violations; and (5) the incentive often is present, on the part of litigants who have a choice between a state court and a federal court for redress of grievances, to choose the federal court.

Thus at least one important, pragmatic purpose is to be adduced for the project in which we are engaged. Although the differentiation of "constitutional violations" from "nonconstitutional violations" may have little significance for state court subject matter jurisdiction, it has great significance for the measurement of federal court subject matter jurisdiction. Our project in this book bears directly upon this important inquiry.

Before constitutional violations may be differentiated from nonconstitutional violations of law within these basic pathologies, however, another question—perhaps a deeper question—must first be explored. The question is: Whom does the Constitution command? This question is the principal subject of our inquiry.

Whom does the U.S. Constitution command? This question bedevils courts and commentators whenever it is expressly posed. And, perhaps for that reason, it is almost never expressly posed.[3]

Whom does the Constitution command? Failure of our U.S. Supreme Court to answer this question with cogency and clarity has spawned a multiplicity of seemingly inconsistent and often incomprehensible decisions that, taken together at least, have lacked even the minimal coherence of consistent pigeonholing. Thus:

Many Supreme Court decisions that have implicitly answered this question have been labeled as "state action" cases, a doctrinal pigeonhole that everyone recognizes to be particularly impenetrable. (A reader who doubts the impenetrability of "state action" doctrine, at least as derived from Supreme Court opinions in which it is given play, should compare *Shelley v. Kraemer* [1948][4] with *Flagg Brothers, Inc. v. Brooks* [1978][5] with *Lugar v. Edmundson Oil Co.* [1982].[6])

At other times this question is addressed, again implicitly, in cases concerning the meaning of "under color of state law" in federal civil rights statutes. (This doctrinal area likewise is terribly confusing; compare *Monroe v. Pape* [1961][7] with *Parratt v. Taylor* [1981][8] with *Pembaur v. City of Cincinnati* [1986].[9])

At still other times this question is implicated in cases that deal with the "torts" of government officials and with the relevance of state remedial law. (This doctrinal area is also confusing; compare *Monroe v. Pape* [1961][10] with *Logan v. Zimmerman Brush Co.* [1982][11] with *Davidson v. Cannon* [1986].[12])

Finally, this question is a direct concern in the *"Pullman abstention"* cases, which are treated as doctrinally far afield from the previous groups we have mentioned. (Once more, the doctrines in this area are confusing; compare *Reetz v. Bozanich* (1970)[13] with *Hawaii Housing Authority v. Midkiff* [1984].[14])

Whom does the Constitution command? Three general alternative answers to this question come immediately to mind:

1. The Constitution commands—imposes prescriptions upon—only those persons who are acting in the role of lawmakers within our federal system. (We will refer to this answer as the "Legalist model.")

2. The Constitution commands not only those persons who are acting in the role of lawmakers, but also a broader audience composed of persons who perform other governmental roles, imposing prescriptions upon them that are linked to their association with government. (We will refer to this answer as the "Governmental model.")

3. The Constitution commands more broadly still, imposing prescriptions upon each person within the jurisdiction of American law, so that each of us might sometime "violate" a constitutionally imposed prescription while acting in a purely private, nongovernmental capacity. (We will refer to this answer as the "Naturalist model.")

These three general answers may be conceived of as shown in Diagram 1.1.

Any choice from among these three alternative answers to the central question, it must be noted, may not operate across the entire range of the Constitution's prescriptions. Particular constitutional provisions, by their terms at least, may command only lawmakers; the "bill of attainder" and "ex post facto law" clauses may furnish examples of such limited commands. Other constitutional provisions may specifically command particular governmental officials; perhaps the Third Amendment (quartering of soldiers) is a good example of such a command. Still other constitutional provisions—the Thirteenth Amendment (involuntary servitude) comes immediately to mind—may command generally, with an ambiguous target audience.

Thus, the inquiry in which we are engaged, at least by hypothesis, is unlikely to invite the selection of a single answer from among the alternatives we have identified to cover the entire range of constitutional prescriptions. The promise would seem to be that a single answer from among these alternatives is properly in order with respect to each of the Constitution's prescriptions.

Whatever the promise may be within our general inquiry, we do not intend in this book to attempt to answer the central question—Whom does

DIAGRAM 1.1
THE AMBIT OF THE CONSTITUTION'S COMMANDS (?)

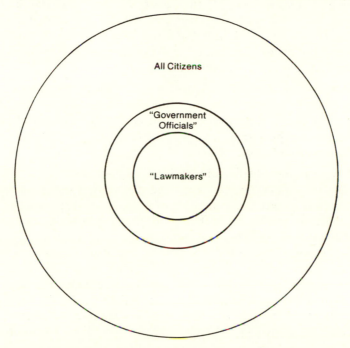

the Constitution command?—for the Constitution as a whole, or indeed for any particular constitutional provision. Nor do we intend to discuss the substantive values that ultimately are implicated in the realm of constitutional litigation that is within this question's compass.

Instead, our purpose is conceptual, analytical, and exegetical in character, not argumentative or normative. Formally, at least, we will take no position with respect to which model, from among the three we have introduced above, ultimately should be preferred with respect to any particular constitutional provision or with respect to the Constitution taken as a whole. We take issue, not with the results of any particular case or group of cases, but rather with the conceptual morass that has been created by failure to deal explicitly with the central question we have posed.

What seems remarkable to us, then, is that after all these years of constitutional interpretation and adjudication, we still have so much room for straightforward exegetical inquiry with respect to the question we have made the central project of this book.

Although our task is conceptual analysis, rather than prescription, undoubtedly our analysis is fraught with prescriptive implications. For example, we are agreed:

One model—the one we have dubbed the "Governmental model"—
and its variants is an unprincipled model, with nothing to recommend
its acceptance other than (1) the possibility that particular, narrow
provisions in the Constitution seem comfortably to prescribe it, or (2)
more generally, the possibility that it furnishes a compromise of sorts
between the more extreme and principled "Legalist" and
"Naturalist" models we have identified.

"Hybrids" that might be constructed by combining two of our
three "pure" models (that is, "Legalist/Naturalist," "Legalist/
Governmental," "Governmental/Naturalist") are theoretical possi-
bilities but also theoretical monsters, perhaps even less principled than
the Governmental model.

As between the Legalist and Naturalist models, one or the other—
but not both—ought articulately to be settled upon as the presumptively correct answer to the question of constitutional referent, at least
on a constitutional-provision-by-constitutional-provision basis.

We do not take sides, in this book, with respect to the question whether
the Legalist model or the Naturalist model should be settled upon, for two
sufficient reasons. One reason is that we disagree about the relative and
comparative merits and demerits of each of these models. The other reason
may be related to the first, but need not be: Our purpose in this book is
nonprescriptive, analytical, exegetical. The prescriptions will come, we are
sure, only after the conceptual analysis and exegesis are articulated.

Thus our aim in this book is immodest yet limited. Our aim is to bring
order, in the abstract at least, to the various categories of cases—and the
conceptual morass in which they are mired—that deal with the question of
whom the Constitution commands. Doubtless our aim will miss the mark
with respect to cases decided in the past. However, by fleshing out the
conceptual framework entailed in the question and its answering—in the
three basic models we have identified and in their variants—perhaps the
future will be made a clearer matter.

Our audience for this book is both fairly sophisticated and fairly
extensive. Lawyers, courts, and academics in all fields, if they are generally
familiar with the categories of cases we have identified above—whether or
not they have experienced the vertigo the case law has generated—are likely
candidates for our audience.

One final point before we proceed further. Although we have already
alluded to a handful of cases by name and do so occasionally in the
remainder of this book's text, most of the discussion in the text will be
devoid of explicit reference to particular cases or even particular constitutional provisions.

We realize the difficulty that this apparently abstract manner of discussion presents, but we ask the reader's indulgence.[15] No case can be understood in terms of our models until all the models have been presented and their implications explored. Why that is so itself cannot be understood in advance of understanding all the models. And the text of this book contains nothing beyond explication of the models. The reader will find ample treatment of the cases in the two appendices that appear after the text's conclusion.

We turn, then, to the three basic models that furnish answers to the question of whom the Constitution commands, and to some variants of these basic models. We shall articulate each model, note its strengths and weaknesses, identify its implications, and describe roughly the extent to which the model squares with prior case law. (A much more thorough analysis of the case law as it pertains to the models is to be found in Appendix A.)

PART I _____

Three Models of the Constitution and Its Referents

We have introduced our central question and the three general models for its answering: Does the Constitution command only lawmakers (our "Legalist model"), all government officials whether or not they are lawmakers (our "Governmental model"), or all citizens generally, including all governmental officials (our "Naturalist model")? Before turning to exegesis, we state our theses with respect to these three abstract models and their interrelationships:

1. The choice from among these models has no bearing on who should prevail on the substantive merits of any lawsuit. If someone has a claim with substantive merit, he or she will prevail—or will not prevail—regardless of the model that is understood to govern. Rather, the choice among these models affects only nonsubstantive aspects of lawsuits: how the substantive claim is characterized, what the grounds of decision are with respect to the claim, against whom the primary claim is to be asserted, and where (sometimes when) the claim may be asserted.

For example, the choice among these models affects the determination whether, given a particular substantive claim, that claim is a federal constitutional claim or is instead only a nonconstitutional (state law or federal statutory law) claim, or whether the lawsuit in which the claim is asserted belongs within the concurrent jurisdiction of the federal courts as opposed to the exclusive jurisdiction of the state courts.

2. Theoretically at least, both the Legalist model and the Governmental model maintain a firm distinction between federal constitu-

tional and nonconstitutional grounds for decision, and hence between federal court and state court jurisdiction over at least some claims. The Naturalist model, on the other hand, collapses these distinctions.

Put differently: The Constitution itself—by virtue of its limited referent—furnishes a basis for keeping litigants out of federal court according to the Legalist model and Governmental model; not so—by virtue of its unlimited referent—according to the Naturalist model.

3. The Legalist model and the Naturalist model are theoretically more coherent and more defensible than is the Governmental model.

Because the two extreme models exhibit greater theoretical integrity, we will deal with them before turning to the intermediate Governmental model.

2

The Legalist Model

THE MODEL DESCRIBED

The Legalist model is arguably in accord both with some common notions of what constitutions are about and with the assumptions of our Constitution's authors about the nature of their document. The premise of this model is that the focus of constitutional prescriptions is a sovereignty's legal regime. The question of whether there has been a violation of the Constitution is interpreted in the following way:

> The Constitution (or one of its provisions) either mandates the existence of a particular legal regime, prohibits the existence of a particular legal regime, or permits a limited number of alternative legal regimes.[1]
>
> The legal regime that is called into question is either on or off the list of legal regimes that are mandated or permitted by the Constitution.
>
> If the legal regime called into question is off the list of mandated or permitted legal regimes, then the Constitution has been violated.

A "legal regime," for purposes of the Legalist model, is a sovereign's entire set of laws (excluding the Constitution itself), rather than any particular law within the set.[2] Thus, for example, a legal regime's remedial laws—those specifying who is liable and to what extent for violation of other laws—are integral parts of the legal regime in question; and both the regime's duty-imposing laws and the regime's remedial laws are part of the entire set of laws that is to be evaluated in a constitutional case.[3] Moreover, a given sovereignty's legal regime includes not only the entire set of laws on its books—constitutional, statutory, administrative, judge-made—but includes as well the unwritten rules, policies, and practices by which the written laws are implemented and the resources allocated to their implementation. Theoretically, a Herculean observer who accepted the Legalist model's criteria for identifying a sovereignty's legal regime could produce a complete description of that legal regime at any given moment in time.[4]

Thus the Constitution's referent, according to the Legalist model, is not people and their activities generally, but rather lawmaking and laws—whole sets of laws, or legal regimes. Put differently, the Constitution is a set of laws that governs, prescribes for, and validates or invalidates other sets of laws that are nonconstitutional in character. If a nonconstitutional set of laws—the legal regime of a sovereignty (excluding the Constitution itself)—is not one of the sets of laws permitted by the Constitution, then the nonconstitutional set of laws is unconstitutional and invalid.

Perhaps our linguistic articulation of the Legalist model is enhanced by the representation of the model shown in Diagram 2.1.

DIAGRAM 2.1
THE LEGALIST MODEL I

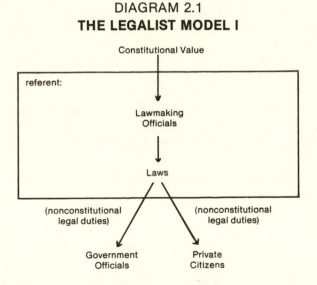

PROBLEMS WITHIN THE LEGALIST MODEL: DEFINING "LAW"

The characteristic of the Legalist model that is its strength is also its weakness. The Legalist model is characterized by the drawing of a solid line between "laws" (sets of laws, or legal regimes) and "other things." The line thus drawn, the model identifies the Constitution's referent to be "laws" and not "other things."

The problem, of course, is in the line drawing. What constitutes a "law" (set of laws, or legal regime) as opposed to an "other thing"? This problem reposes *within* the Legalist model itself; it must be resolved before the model can achieve cogency and internal consistency on its own terms. This central problem has many variants, some of which we briefly identify here:

Who Are the "Lawmakers"?

Identification of the "lawmakers"—those who have authority to create "laws"—is a necessary task for resolution of the line between "law" and "other things." Only a "lawmaker, while acting in the role of lawmaker," has the ability to make "laws." One who is not a "lawmaker acting in the role of lawmaker" can never be credited with "having made a law" for purposes of the operation of the Legalist model.

Although understandable in the abstract, this aspect of distinguishing "laws" from "other things" is fraught with difficulty. The difficulty has to do with the methodology by which the definition of "lawmaker" is accomplished. Who or what—some institution *inside* the relevant legal regime (such as a state legislature, or a state constitution), or something *outside* the relevant legal regime (such as the Constitution itself, or perhaps a particular theory of jurisprudence)—has control over the definition of "lawmaker" within that legal regime?

Suppose, for example, that a state constitution clearly distinguished between "legislative power" and "judicial power," and then went on to assert that (1) only those endowed with "legislative power" could make laws, and (2) those endowed with "judicial power" were precluded from exercising "legislative power." Then would all exercises of "judicial power"—decisions by courts in particular cases—be excluded, by that legal regime's definition, from the concept of "laws" upon which the Legalist model operates?

It seems doubtful that, for federal constitutional purposes, a state could simply stipulate a test for identification of its "laws" and then have that test be treated as conclusive for purposes of the determination of federal constitutional issues. True, legal positivism in a general sense identifies law with norms deemed by "officials" to be proper bases for coercion. True as well that "officials" are usually identified by legal tests drawn from the very legal regime in question.[5] Ultimately, however, if vicious circularity is to be avoided, the "officials" who are "lawmakers" must be subject to extralegal identification—for example, as those whose pronouncements are treated as authoritative by most people most of the time. Once so identified, the "officials" then can be looked to for identification of the "lawmakers acting in their role of lawmakers," who can in turn be looked to for identification of "laws." But as anyone who has struggled within legal positivism can attest, attempts to identify "laws" through this method are at the very least extremely messy and at worst quite arbitrary.

What Counts for a "Law"?

Surely there are things that, when invoked or implicated in particular situations, would be conceded to be "laws" by everyone. The Legalist, however, defines the boundaries of her model in terms of whether something is or is not a "law"; and conceded exemplars of "law" cannot provide a satisfactory resolution of the model's boundary.

Previously we suggested that, by referring to a government's entire legal regime, the Legalist model would incorporate within its ambit a wide variety of "laws": constitutional provisions, statutory enactments, administrative regulations, judge-made rules, and perhaps as well an indefinite array of unwritten rules, policies, and practices by which "recorded laws" are implemented. Such a broad definition of "laws," while perfectly understandable in the abstract and entirely consistent with honest employment of the Legalist model, creates havoc for the thoroughgoing Legalist's attempts at line drawing.

Suppose, for example, that a state statute gives an administrative official discretion to do either A or B as the situation warrants, and the official determines to "do A not B" in a particular situation. Is the determination to "do A not B"—or, indeed, to "do A not B in the particular situation"—to be included within, or to be excluded from, the concept of "laws" for purposes of the operation of the Legalist model?

A thoroughgoing Legalist would be concerned with such a question. If the tentative conclusion is that such exercises of administrative discretion count as "lawmaking"—and any other conclusion by a Legalist seems untenable to us—then the Legalist confronts a very basic difficulty in attempts to mark her model's boundary. Many—perhaps most—laws delegate discretion, not only to government officials, but also to private citizens. The "laws" we associate with "property" and "contract," for example, principally serve to define and channel private discretion. Is the exercise of this discretion—the "private ordering" that in its effects on others closely resembles the public ordering of law—"lawmaking"? If so, then the boundary between the Legalist and other models is seriously compromised. If not, then we need to know why not, how not, and when not; and any attempt to resolve this problem by resort to a model's need for clear boundaries is unlikely to assuage our need to know.[6]

The *Pembaur* Case: An Illustration

Pembaur v. City of Cincinnati (1986),[7] illustrates the intersection of the two problems within the Legalist model that we have discussed: Who are the

"lawmakers"? and what counts for a "law"? In that case, the defendant
county was liable only if the decision by various county officials to conduct
a particular search and seizure was tantamount to a "law." The Supreme
Court itself did not decide the issue, but instead remanded the case to the
lower courts after a very general discussion of "lawmaking" by
administrative officials.

Similar issues arise whenever administrators make *ad hoc* decisions that
are neither explicitly authorized nor explicitly forbidden by more
paradigmatic "laws," and where, if those decisions are deemed "laws,"
they are unconstitutional. Even the presence of a law authorizing
compensation to persons injured by such administrative decisions does not
clearly resolve their status.[8] First, sometimes administrators are legally
authorized to injure others in certain ways and then to pay just
compensation—for example, where the administrator engages in an
authorized taking of property. Second, as the discussion below of
"inconsistent laws" illustrates, one might wish to deem certain decisions by
administrators to be "lawmaking" even if explicitly forbidden by higher-
order laws.

The Problem of "Invalid Laws"

It might be thought that, once a definition of "law" is satisfactorily
achieved, then problems for the Legalist model will be completely resolved.
However, consider the common reference to things called "invalid laws."
We commonly distinguish—and probably must be able to distinguish—
between the *existence* of a "law" (or set of laws) and the *invalidity* of a
"law" (or set of laws). But can the Legalist model operate with such a
distinction?

The problem is that the Constitution functions not only as a set of
prescriptions for lawmakers, but also as part of the "rule of recognition"
by which other laws are identified. Perhaps another way of stating the same
thing is that the Constitution is not an alien document to the legal regimes
within its ambit, but rather is incorporated implicitly into those legal
regimes. Then, from this perspective, there could never be an "unconstitutional law" or "unconstitutional legal regime." That is so because a rule
that was constitutionally invalid could not be recognized to be a "law"; it
would, instead, be some "other thing."

If this analysis is correct, then the Legalist model leads us to run around
the following circle:

1. The Constitution's referent is legal regimes composed of laws, and
   not other things.
2. Invalid laws are "other things," not "laws."
3. Therefore, there is no such thing as an "unconstitutional law" or

"unconstitutional legal regime"; instead, there are only other things that, if they were laws, would be unconstitutional.

4. "Other things," however, are not included within the Constitution's referent.

5. (Proceed back to 2 and then go around the circle again, as frequently as you wish.)

The result of this circularity within the operation of the Legalist model would be that the realm of constitutional litigation would be entirely dissolved, at least as we know it today. Today we have claims presented for adjudication that laws are unconstitutional, and we have adjudications that those laws are or are not unconstitutional. If the Legalist model were applied rigorously, however, then constitutional litigation would commence by a party's raising of the issue that a "law" (or set of "laws") relevant to the litigation was unconstitutional. This issue, however, could never be addressed frontally. Instead:

The first inquiry would be whether the alleged "law" was actually a law or instead was some other thing.

The determination of this inquiry would be coextensive with the determination of constitutionality. The determination that the alleged "law" was actually a law would entail the determination that the alleged "law" was not unconstitutional. The determination that the alleged "law" was "unconstitutional if it were a law" would entail the determination that the alleged "law" was not actually a law, but rather was some other thing.

The determination that the alleged "law" was actually some other thing—that is, something that, if it were a law, would be unconstitutional—would eliminate the adjudicator's jurisdiction to determine constitutional issues.[9]

The problem raised here can be traced to the Constitution's characteristic as both a power-conferring and duty-imposing instrument. As a power-conferring instrument, the Constitution functions as a test of legal validity and defines the conditions for making laws. As a duty-imposing instrument— construed according to the Legalist model—the Constitution mandates that lawmakers refrain from making invalid laws.[10]

Given this opening analysis, it would appear that the Legalist model ultimately requires an intermediate notion—between "laws" and "other things"—in order to take account of "invalid laws" without dissolving into an extended tautology. Such an intermediate notion likely would function within the following mechanism for constitutional litigation:

Suppose temporarily that the Constitution (or at least its provision that is placed in issue) does not apply to the legal regime in question.

Then determine whether the thing in question is part of the legal regime in question; that is, determine whether the thing is a "law." If so, then the thing in question is an "apparent law."

Then insert the following premise (our "intermediate notion"): "Apparent laws," thus determined, are given the status of "law" for purposes of constitutional adjudication.

Now reinsert the Constitution and its applicability into the legal regime in question.

Application of this mechanism would commence with the allegation that "if X is a law, then X is unconstitutional." The determination of this allegation would proceed: (a) if X is an apparent law, then X is a law for purposes of constitutional adjudication; (b) X is an apparent law; (c) if X were a law, then X would be unconstitutional; (d) X is unconstitutional. Put differently, the Constitution speaks to those things that would be laws of the legal regime in question *either* if there were no Constitution *or* if the challenge to their constitutionality is unsuccessful.

The Legalist can thus solve the problem of distinguishing "laws" from "other things" for purposes of her model by introducing the notion of "apparent laws," things that would be laws but for their federal unconstitutionality. That still leaves the Legalist with the thorny problems of defining "laws," upon which the notion of "apparent laws" is dependent. But the Legalist is at least spared the embarrassment of constructing a model whose referent—unconstitutional "laws"—is a null set.

The Problem of "Inconsistent Laws"

Even if a thoroughgoing Legalist could construct the calculus that would surmount the problems we have identified thus far—problems that, in the main, are addressed to the definition of the "legal regime" to which the Constitution refers—yet another difficulty is presented for the Legalist model. This difficulty relates to the problem of internally inconsistent "laws" that are discovered to repose within a stipulated legal regime.

In order to pretend to cogency, the Legalist model must identify the criteria by which acts by officials (or others) that *establish* legal norms are to be distinguished from acts by officials (or others) that *transgress* legal norms.[11] Some such criteria undoubtedly will be provided within a particular legal regime: for example, by higher-level legal norms that are accepted by the officials (or others) themselves. These internal criteria comfortably will assist in the determination whether a particular act entails the establishment of a legal norm or the transgression of a preexisting legal norm. For constitutional purposes, however, the Legalist model demands its own criteria for making tnis determination; otherwise unconstitutional transgressions (those that, according to the Legalist, relate to the establishment of legal norms) cannot clearly be distinguished from nonconstitutional transgressions (those that relate to the violation of legal norms that are themselves not unconstitutional).[12] And precious little if anything within the Constitution itself, so far as we can tell, can be found to supply the Legalist with these criteria.

Consider the following examples that seem to entail this conceptual problem of characterizing acts of officials (and others) as "lawmaking" rather than as "illegal": acts that are legally proscribed and subject to sanction, but are not resistible by ordinary citizens;[13] illegal, sanctionable, and perhaps completely resistible acts of officials who possess the "pretense" of authority for such acts;[14] acts, such as erroneous lower court decisions, that are proscribed (by being reversible by higher authority) but are subject neither to sanction nor to resistance by ordinary citizens;[15] acts of officials that are neither explicitly proscribed nor explicitly authorized but for which the state provides a damages remedy;[16] acts of officials that are neither explicitly proscribed nor explicitly authorized and for which the state (permissibly) provides no damages remedy;[17] and state laws that violate the state's own constitution (or other higher-order state laws) but that nevertheless are on the books.[18]

In a similar vein, consider the state statute or administrative regulation that, although it is formally "on the books," is never actually enforced despite its frequent violation.[19] The Legalist model must confront the question whether such an unenforced statute or regulation is a "law."

THE NEED TO EXAMINE ALTERNATIVE MODELS

The main strength of the Legalist model is in the boundary it permits us to draw between violations of *constitutional* prescriptions—and the source of those violations—and violations of only *nonconstitutional* prescriptions. This strength is drawn from the values—and the assumptions that are erected upon those values—that are associated with a federal system, in which subset legal regimes (the states) are accorded a substantial measure of sovereignty.

The problems we have identified with the internal workings of the Legalist model, though formidable, may not be insurmountable.[20] Various more or less arbitrary devices may be employed to resolve these problems, in order to maintain the integrity both of the model and of the state-law/federal-constitutional-law boundary within the Constitution's domain. We have suggested a couple of these devices in the preceding discussion; and, in that discussion, we have also suggested some of the difficulties that attend the articulation and deployment of these devices.

It may seem to many readers that, despite its difficulties, the Legalist model *is* the obviously correct model for answering the question of whom the Constitution commands. These readers will consider it beyond cavil that the Constitution governs nonconstitutional "laws," and that the bearers of constitutional duties are the "lawmakers." If so, then they may see no need for examining other possible models; instead, they will set about the task of shoring up the Legalist model from within.

Nevertheless, we follow the impulse to examine other models—an impulse generated not only by the internal theoretical difficulties of the Legalist model, but also by intellectual curiosity concerning what those other models hold in store. And ardent Legalists, too, do well to engage in this examination. There would seem to be some pressing practical reasons to engage in such an examination. We proffer two practical reasons here.

First there is the plain and practical observation that a number of Supreme Court decisions appear to reject the Legalist model as the governing *ratio decidendi* (sometimes, it must be admitted, over violent dissent).

The landmark cases of *Monroe v. Pape* (1961)[21] and *Screws v. United States* (1945)[22] are classic examples of decisions that fit more comfortably with models other than the Legalist model. In those cases, governmental officials did not "enact" unconstitutional laws, at least not in any sense a Legalist would find comfortable. Instead, they violated state laws that were constitutionally adequate. Yet the Supreme Court declared that constitutional rights were violated in both cases and offered a federal forum that otherwise would have been unavailable but for the alleged constitutional violation. The coexistence of those nonLegalist-model decisions with the more recent Legalist-model decisions in *Parratt v. Taylor* (1981),[23] *Hudson v. Palmer* (1984),[24] *Daniels v. Williams* (1986),[25] and *Davidson v. Cannon* (1986)[26] has spawned considerable confusion.

Moreover, in *Lugar v. Edmundson Oil Co.* (1982),[27] the Supreme Court held that private invocation of an unconstitutional legal procedure was itself unconstitutional "state action," a result that, superficially at least, is inconsistent with the Legalist model. On another front, in several cases in which federal courts were asked to abstain from rendering a constitutional decision until after determination of the validity of a challenged law under a relevant state constitution, the Supreme Court has deemed abstention to have been improper,[28] again in apparent contradiction of the predicted result under the Legalist model.[29]

The Supreme Court also has held that acts of state officials, illegal on state law grounds, are nonetheless acts of the "state" for purposes of the

Eleventh Amendment.[30] Such a result, while not necessarily inconsistent with the Legalist model—since the Eleventh Amendment does not impose duties on state lawmakers—at least must be conceded to sit ill-at-ease with that model for the Constitution's referent.

Even when the Supreme Court reaches results that are consistent with the Legalist model, it often confuses the issue of choice of model with substantive issues that have absolutely no part to play in that choice. Illustrations of this confusion are abundant, the most significant of which may be found in the morass known as "state action."[31] A little discussion here about "state action" may serve to whet the appetite for examination of alternative models.

The "state action" doctrine is, on its own terms, completely incoherent. The doctrine's design is to eliminate from the realm of constitutional claims those claims that do not involve "state action." However, all acts—no matter how trivial, and no matter by whom taken—have a legal status: they are either legally forbidden, legally mandated, or legally permitted.[32] It follows that any constitutional challenge to a particular act can be reformulated in terms of a constitutional challenge to the laws of the state that govern the act. If anything is "state action," then the laws of the state are. All laws of a state are equally laws, and hence are equally "state action." Therefore, "state action" cannot serve as a limitation on constitutional claims.

Nevertheless—a matter well known to the most casual student of constitutional law—the Supreme Court continues, term after term, to behave as though the "state action requirement" really *is* a limitation on the presentation of constitutional claims. Since "state action" cannot serve as a limitation, the Court must be confusing the (non)issue of "state action" with other issues.

Then what are those other issues that are being confused with "state action"? One issue (or set of issues) has to do with the substantive merits of the constitutional claim in question: Frequently the Supreme Court invokes "state action" as another (and incoherent) way of saying that the object of complaint is not unconstitutional on the merits, all things considered; but better, in these instances, to declare the merits directly than by resort to "state action" rhetoric. A second issue, however, is more telling here: Frequently the Supreme Court has confused "state action" with the issue of who should be sued, on what grounds, and in what court. This second issue goes, not to the substantive merits, but rather to the question of whom the Constitution commands.

We will return to the "state action" conundrum in Chapter 9. Suffice it here to hold any impatient Legalists in our audience: In order to understand fully the question of whom the Constitution commands, one must examine not just one model, but rather a range of alternative models, with which the question may be answered. Perhaps the Legalist model, though fraught with complexity, turns out to be the best of available models. Perhaps, however, another model will better meet the test of Occam's Razor without raising new difficulties. Thus, we turn to the other models.

One transitional note. The reader should keep in mind that each of the following models includes the domain of the Legalist model within it, and has the effect of revising outward the external boundary of the Legalist domain. That is, any act that would be held to violate the Constitution on the Legalist model also necessarily will be held to violate the Constitution on the other models we will examine, although the converse of this statement is not necessarily true. As we previously have indicated, the three principal models relate to one another like three concentric circles. The Legalist model occupies the innermost circle; the Naturalist model occupies the outermost circle; and the Governmental model occupies an intermediate circle. (After examining briefly the Naturalist and Governmental models, we will take up three hybrid models that combine aspects of two or more of the main models in a nonconcentric way.)

3

The Naturalist Model

The Naturalist model produces a simple and direct answer to the question of whom the Constitution commands. Its answer is that the Constitution, which is the "supreme law of the land" in a society that draws no clear line between "law" and "other things," commands everyone within that society's jurisdiction. Such an answer, of course, avoids the difficulties that arise in attempts to create a more restricted audience for the Constitution's referent. In avoiding these difficulties, the Naturalist model poses a new set of difficulties that relate primarily to the maintenance of a federalist regime and of clear jurisdictional boundaries between state and federal governments.

THE MODEL DESCRIBED

According to the Naturalist model, the Constitution mandates, forbids, and permits various states of affairs, not just in the law itself, but also in the world that law governs. That is, the Constitution speaks directly to all acts, whether those acts amount to lawmaking or law applying, whether they can be acts that only governmental officials can commit, or otherwise.

According to other models for the Constitution's referent, the Constitution speaks only indirectly to acts undertaken by private citizens. That is so because the other models maintain the Constitution speaks only to the laws, or perhaps to laws and governmental officials, that in turn act on private citizens to mandate, prohibit, or permit "private acts." The Naturalist model rejects this two-step procedure. If an act, whether by an official or by a private citizen, violates a norm that the Constitution prescribes, then the actor has engaged directly in a constitutional violation according to the Naturalist model.

Thus, if the Constitution requires that the states have laws against murder and theft, then it is so because acts of murder and theft are bad things constitutionally; and they would be bad things constitutionally regardless whether they were also made illegal under the (nonconstitutional) laws of the state. Or if the Constitution forbids that a state permit certain types of creditor repossession, then any act of creditor repossession within the constitutional prohibition, even if it happens also to be illegal under the laws of the state, amounts to a constitutional violation by the creditor.

Perhaps our linguistic articulation of the Naturalist model is enhanced by the representation of the model shown in Diagram 3.1, which then may be compared with our previous diagram of the Legalist model.

DIAGRAM 3.1
THE NATURALIST MODEL I

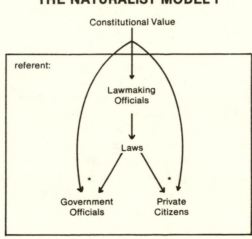

* constitutional as well as nonconstitutional
  duties with respect to the same acts

DIFFICULTIES WITH THE NATURALIST MODEL: PRESERVING A LIMITED FEDERAL JURISDICTION

The major difficulty with the Naturalist model lies in its conversion of every claim of illegality under state and local law into a federal constitutional claim, so long as the Constitution would proscribe a state's or local government's legalization of the act that is the subject of the claim.[1]

Thus, suppose the contracts clause of the Constitution requires that the state must proscribe and provide a remedy for a private breach of contract, at least whenever the law of the state at the time of contracting proscribed breach and provided for a remedy. Or suppose the due process clause requires that a state must proscribe and provide a remedy for certain categories of injury-imposing acts by private citizens.[2] On the Naturalist model, a promisor who breaches such a promise, or a private citizen who engages in such an injury-imposing act, has violated the Constitution in addition to having violated any law of the state and being subject to the state's remedial laws.[3] On the Legalist model, by contrast, something unconstitutional has occurred only when the lawmakers have failed to proscribe and provide adequate remedies for the private acts; and it is only the lawmakers—and not the private individuals—who will be deemed to have acted unconstitutionally.

Now it may be contended that the difficulty we have introduced here is not a difficulty at all in most instances. So far as actions brought in state courts are concerned, or actions brought in federal courts in which jurisdiction may be predicated on theories other than federal constitutional violations, the Naturalist model would do little more than to suggest a rephrasing of claim (or defense) in federal constitutional as well as nonconstitutional terms. Just so, if our analysis of the Naturalist model—what it does not do as well as what it does—is accurate.

The difficulty with the Naturalist model lies in its implications with respect to those instances in which federal-court original jurisdiction is understood to be available only if a federal constitutional claim is asserted. In these instances the Naturalist model invites havoc. Given current understanding of the contours of federal court original jurisdiction, the contract breacher, the injury imposer, and the murderer, thief, and repossessor in our previous illustrations all have violated the Constitution and thus are potentially subject to suit in federal district court by those claiming against them. The claimant, on the Naturalist model, has a federal cause of action.[4]

Here it should be noted that the difficulty we identify here is not necessarily a matter of the internal operations of the Naturalist model. The original jurisdiction of the lower federal courts is not necessarily the product of federal constitutional mandate. State courts have original jurisdiction over federal constitutional claims wherever federal district courts have similar jurisdiction; and the original jurisdiction of the federal district courts may well be subject to statutory control.[5] Nevertheless, there is intuitive validity in the notion that federal courts have jurisdiction to determine federal constitutional claims. Thus the main difficulty with the Naturalist model remains.

4

The Governmental Model

The Legalist model gives us one extreme version of the Constitution's referent. This model conceives of the Constitution as the highest level of legal norms, which operate on all lower-level legal norms. Employment of the Legalist model thus requires us to distinguish between lower-level legal norms and other things. Creation of such a distinction, we have suggested, entails a very messy enterprise.

The Naturalist model gives us the other extreme version of the Constitution's referent. This model conceives of the Constitution as the highest level of legal norms, which operate on all acts (including not only lower-level legal norms but also the acts of private citizens). Employment of the Naturalist model, we have suggested, creates some pretty extreme implications for the prevailing boundaries of federal court original jurisdiction.

The Governmental model gives us a version of the Constitution's referent that lies intermediate between the Legalist model and the Naturalist model. Its strengths lie in its attempts to meet the difficulties posed by the extremes, largely by expanding upon the boundaries of the Legalist model. Its difficulties relate to its inability either to clearly delineate or to justify the intermediate boundary it posits for the Constitution's referent.

THE MODEL DESCRIBED

According to the Governmental model for the Constitution's referent, the Constitution is the highest level of legal norms, which operate, not just on lower-level legal norms (the Legalist model), but also on some of the nonlawmaking activities of persons who comprise "the government."

The Governmental model is distinguished from the Legalist model as follows. On the Legalist model, if all lower-level legal norms are in accord with the Constitution, then governmental officials (acting in their capacities as "lawmakers") have fulfilled their constitutional obligations; thereafter these and other governmental officials may very well act illegally, but their illegal acts do not amount to constitutional violations, since those acts are not "lawmaking." On the Governmental model, however, governmental officials perform various constitutionally relevant government functions besides simply "lawmaking"; and any act by a governmental official that (1) contravenes any nonconstitutional law demanded by the Constitution, whether or not "lawmaking" and despite its illegality under the legal regime in question, or that (2) could not be permitted by a constitutionally proper legal regime, would also be an unconstitutional act if it occurs while the official is acting within her "official capacity."[1]

The Governmental model likewise is to be distinguished from the Naturalist model. Unlike the Naturalist model, the Governmental model maintains that an act committed by a private citizen (including a government official acting outside her "official capacity") is not an unconstitutional act, and hence not a constitutional violation, even if it (1) contravenes a nonconstitutional law demanded by the Constitution or (2) would be impermissible under a constitutionally proper legal regime.

Perhaps our linguistic articulation of the Governmental model is enhanced by the representation of the model shown in Diagram 4.1, which then may be compared with our previous diagrams of the Legalist and Naturalist models.

DIFFICULTIES WITH THE GOVERNMENTAL MODEL: DEFINING "GOVERNMENT OFFICIAL" . . . "ACTING IN OFFICIAL CAPACITY"

The Governmental model—a model that the Supreme Court appears at times to follow—shares definitional difficulties with the Legalist model.[2] The main conceptual difficulties with the Governmental model, however, arise along the boundaries between "government officials" and "private citizens."

Who Is an "Official"?

The Legalist model needs a definition for "lawmaker." The Governmental model needs, as well, a definition for "government official."

As we have suggested previously, many legal regimes furnish their own definitions for what constitutes their "government officials"; such definitions, even if taken to be complete, cannot be considered to bind the courts where matters of constitutional claim are at stake. And, if only those

DIAGRAM 4.1
THE GOVERNMENTAL MODEL I

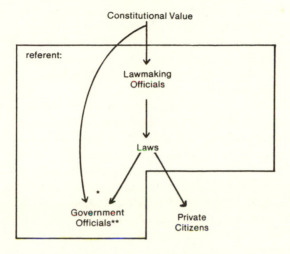

Constitutional Value

referent:

Lawmaking
Officials

Laws

Government
Officials**

Private
Citizens

---

* constitutional as well as nonconstitutional
  duties with respect to the same acts

** ... "acting in their official capacity"
   (otherwise, treated as "private citizens")

persons with the legal power to determine conclusively or to change law are understood to be "government officials" (when and only when they are acting in their lawmaking capacity), then the Governmental model simply collapses back into the Legalist model (as well as into the Legalist model's difficulties). (Conversely, if all acts of government officials—even those that are illegal—that are deemed to be within their official capacities are also deemed to entail "lawmaking," then the Legalist model has simply been expanded to include the Governmental model.)[3]

However, if government officials are defined more broadly to include persons who are not acting in the role of "lawmakers," then a serious problem arises. We have no available criteria for defining "government officials" in a way that will serve to distinguish them from "private citizens" in terms of capacity to be sued on a federal constitutional claim in a federal court. Put differently, the Governmental model places far too great a premium on government employment to prove a satisfactory answer for the question of the Constitution's referent. A minor bureaucrat who violates state or local law hardly seems different in any constitutionally significant sense from a private citizen who does the same, even if in both instances the violated law is one demanded by the Constitution, and even if the bureaucrat is acting within the scope of her government employment when she violates the law.

This point deserves elaboration. The Governmental model includes the Legalist model. The Legalist model imposes a constitutional obligation on government officials to enact and enforce the laws that are required by the Constitution, which is something that only government officials *qua* government officials can do. The Governmental model imposes the same constitutional obligation on government officials, but it goes further. The Governmental model also imposes a constitutional obligation on governmental officials to abide by those laws—and to ignore unconstitutional laws—which is something that private citizens, as well as government officials *qua* government officials, can do.

The Legalist, then, needs a clear and justified definition of "lawmakers" as distinguished from "other government officials"; but the Governmentalist needs what may be a more difficult definition to articulate and then justify, a definition that distinguishes between "government officials" and "private citizens." As we have suggested in our discussion of the Legalist model, one way in which to build such distinctions would begin by identifying clearly the relevant function that is the target of the Constitution's commands, and then to follow that function into the persons who are discovered to engage in it. With the Legalist model, the function is "lawmaking." With the Governmental model, the function is "action performed while in official capacity."

What is "Acting in Official Capacity"?

Assume, for the benefit of the Governmental model, that we can stipulate who is, and who is not, a "government official." Most government officials are government officials only part of the time; the rest of the time they are spouses, parents, taxpayers, automobile drivers, Presbyterians, club and union members—in short, most of the time they are indistinguishable from "private citizens" even according to the Governmental model. According to the Governmental model, government officials may violate constitutional duties only while they are acting in their capacities as government officials; otherwise, they are ordinary folks who can only behave illegally, not unconstitutionally.

It follows that the Governmental model needs a good test by which to distinguish, not only between "government official" and "private citizen," but also between "government official acting in official capacity" and "government official not acting in official capacity." Various tests have been suggested in the case law and commentary for creating this distinction between "(unconstitutional) illegal acts by government officials (acting as government officials)" and "(nonconstitutional) illegal acts by private citizens (including government officials not acting as government officials).''[4] These efforts all boil down to variants of three tests, none of which appears to be satisfactory in accomplishing its intended purpose.[5]

"Pretense of authority." The first test may be labeled "pretense of authority." This test is traceable to Justice Douglas' statement in the majority opinion in *Screws v. United States* (1945):[6] "It is clear that under 'color' of law means under 'pretense' of law."[7]

One problem with the "pretense of authority" test is that its source does not make clear what an act "under pretense of law" is. In *Screws* the defendants, who happened to be police officials, brutally murdered a black prisoner. There was no indication in the case that the defendants ever pretended, either during the murder or afterward, that they had legal authority to commit the murder.

Another, to us fatal, problem with the "pretense" test is that its key is "pretense of authority" not "actual" even "implied" authority. The "pretense" test requires us to examine an illegal act's "officiality-hence-unconstitutionality" from the perspective of those to whom "pretense" appears—victims, onlookers, or strangers (like courts) looking back upon the transaction. The heavy implication is that government officials who are pretending to be private citizens while actually engaged in government business would not come under constitutional commands. The equally heavy implication is that nonofficials, pretending to be officials who are legally authorized to take the actions in question, *would* come under constitutional commands. After all, if "pretense" not "actual" authority is what matters for the Governmental model—as the "pretense of authority" test holds—then it would seem clearly to follow that a rapist who lures his victims by flashing a fake police badge would be the subject of constitutional commands, while a police officer who engages in illegal government surveillance while in plainclothes would be acting beyond the reach of those commands.

"Agency." The second test that has been suggested for purposes of "acting in official capacity" goes like this: A government official will be deemed to be subject to constitutional commands if her acts, despite being illegal, are within the scope of her government employment; and "scope of government employment" is defined according to the common law of agency.

One serious problem with "agency" as the measure of the Governmental model is that no principled test has yet been developed for determining when an agent who is disobeying her principal's orders is still acting on behalf of the principal. We doubt that such a test can be developed, largely because the underlying notion of a legally authorized yet illegal act is incoherent.[8]

A second serious problem with the "agency" test is that its common law design is addressed primarily to questions of the principal's liability, not to questions whether the agent violated a command (constitutional or otherwise). By hypothesis, in most instances in which a government official has violated a constitutionally mandated law, the principal (the state) has not violated the Constitution; instead, it has enacted the law mandated by the Constitution that the agent has violated. The fact that, under agency doctrine, the state as principal might be vicariously liable on constitutional grounds does not prove—but rather assumes to be the case—that the agent was a constitutional duty bearer.[9]

We believe that these problems with the "agency" test—whether taken singly or in combination—present insurmountable barriers for its cogent use in making the Governmental model's crucial distinction between government officials who are, and who are not, subject to the Constitution's commands.

"Abuse of authority." The third test, which we shall label the "abuse of authority" test, derives from Chief Justice White's majority opinion in *Home Telephone & Telegraph Co. v. City of Los Angeles* (1913):[10]

> [T]he settled construction of the [Fourteenth] Amendment is that it presupposes the possibility of an abuse by a state officer or representative of the powers possessed and deals with such a contingency. It provides, therefore, for a case where one who is in possession of state power uses that power to the doing of the wrongs which the Amendment forbids even although the consummation of the wrong may not be within the powers possessed if the commission of the wrong itself is rendered possible or is efficiently aided by the state authority lodged in the wrongdoer. That is to say, the theory of the Amendment is that where an officer or other representative of a State in the exercise of the authority with which he is clothed misuses the power possessed to do a wrong forbidden by the Amendment, inquiry concerning whether the State has authorized the wrong is irrelevant and the Federal judicial power is competent to afford redress for the wrong by dealing with the officer and the result of his exertion of power.[11]

The question becomes: If we assume that the "abuse of authority" test is in fact different from both the "pretense" and "agency" tests—and thus avoids the precise problems that those tests entail—then how are we to go about construing it?

One possibility is to begin by focusing on the "made possible or is efficiently aided" language of *Home Telephone & Telegraph*, and then to argue that government officials—by virtue of that status—are unique in their capacity to harm constitutional values, even when they are acting contrary to state law. The problem with such an argument is that it is just not true.

Sometimes, perhaps, government officials may have a unique capacity, by virtue of their official position, to harm constitutional values. More often, however, their capacity to do so is not unique at all. Moreover, the ability to harm constitutional values through illegal acts that government officials possess by virtue of their legal status, as a general proposition, is no different either in kind or in degree from the ability of private citizens to harm constitutional values through illegal acts that they possess by virtue of *their* legal status and rightful authority. For example, when state laws prohibit self-help remedies and require resort to the courts, private citizens who are wrongfully in possession of the property of others can harm the constitutional values connected with property rights by asserting their legal right to resist self-help attempts and to demand judicial process as a prerequisite of dispossession.[12]

In using the "made possible or is efficiently aided" language, Chief Justice White more likely was asserting that acts of government officials have some presumptive legality under the law, even if those acts turn out to be illegal; and that this presumptive legality poses a special threat to constitutional values because it precludes citizens from resisting or ignoring such acts. After all, the Los Angeles ordinance at issue in *Home Telephone & Telegraph* (which set telephone rates), if in fact illegal under the California Constitution as alleged, *and if entitled to no presumption of legality*, could just as easily be ignored by the telephone company as could an "order" to lower telephone rates that was issued by a private citizen.[13]

The problems with this form of the "abuse of authority" argument, however, are that it proves too little and proves too much. First, not all illegal acts of government officials carry some legal presumption of legality that makes them less easily resisted than ordinary illegal acts can be. Second, some illegal acts of nonofficials carry a similar legal presumption of legality.[14]

Indeed, if the Governmental model is concerned solely with the inclusion of official acts alleged to be an "abuse of authority" within the domain of the Constitution's referent, then the most direct route for the purpose is to include such acts as species of "lawmaking" under the Legalist model.[15] Such a route, if taken, would produce two benefits: First, it would eliminate the Governmental model from further consideration. Second, it would narrow the differences that currently exist, perhaps by virtue of the presence of the Governmental model, between the Legalist model and the Naturalist model.

NULL SETS, FULL SETS, AND THE GOVERNMENTAL MODEL

Now it is conceivable, of course, that particular constitutional provisions require duty-imposing laws that are directed only at government officials.

An illustration of such a provision may be the "cruel and unusual punishment" proscription, which might be understood properly to apply only to government officials.[16]

The presence of such a narrow-based proscription in the Constitution, however, gives no warrant for the presence or employment of the Governmental model as opposed to the Naturalist model. Instead, in the case of these narrowly directed constitutional provisions, it is simply the case that purely private citizens do not have the capacity to violate any legal norm required by the applicable provision. Put differently, "private-citizen violation" is a null category with respect to the constitutional provision in question.[17] In such an instance, the Governmental model would produce the same analytical results as would the Naturalist model; and those analytical results would continue to be at odds with the Legalist model, which would be concerned only with the existence of the requisite legal norms, not with their violation.

On the other hand, take the situation in which laws, required by a constitutional provision, include the imposition of duties on individuals generally, including private citizens and on-duty government officials who are not acting in their capacity as lawmakers. Then the Governmental model will indeed produce results that differ from both of the other models: it labels the violations of those laws by on-duty government officials, but not by private citizens, as unconstitutional acts. Such a result seems to be very problematic.[18]

Thus we conclude: (1) The Governmental model does not succeed in its attempt to provide an acceptable compromise between the principled models, Legalist and Naturalist. (2) The absence of principled foundation for the Governmental model creates insurmountable difficulties that inhere in attempts to apply it cogently. (3) Elimination of the Governmental model from further consideration, at least by the courts, is warranted, either by adding a portion of its ambit to the Legalist model or by leaving its ambit to the Naturalist model.

5

Postscript to the Naturalist and Governmental Models: The Problem of Defining "Unconstitutional Acts"

Our discussion of the Naturalist and Governmental models has treated the notion of an unconstitutional act required by those models as itself unproblematic. But just as under the Legalist model there are difficulties with respect to what count as acts of "lawmaking" and as "laws," so too under the Naturalist and Governmental models there is the analogous difficulty of what count as "unconstitutional acts." Nowhere is this difficulty more apparent than in the area of nonintentional, nonreckless torts committed by private citizens (Naturalist model) or by government officials (both Naturalist and Governmental models).[1]

The area of nonintentional and nonreckless torts is characterized by acts with the following features:

1. The acts injure persons or their property.
2. The acts, by injuring persons or their property, implicate constitutional values.
3. The acts are not punished by fines or imprisonment.
4. The acts, while not expressly authorized, are often not expressly or even impliedly "prohibited." For example, strict or absolute tort liability often attaches to acts that, in a general way, are legally permitted. Or, if the acts are prohibited, the actors are not adverting to the prohibited features at the time.
5. The state provides a damages remedy for those injured by the acts.[2]

Now we know that some acts that meet these conditions are not unconstitutional even if the damages remedy provided is constitutionally compelled. Authorized governmental "takings" are the prominent examples. But what about garden variety nonintentional torts? The actor may have subjectively acted quite reasonably, with proper regard for all constitutional values. In hindsight, after someone is injured, we may regret that the actor acted as she did; and the relevant constitutional values may compel the state to provide a damages remedy. Does it follow that the actor acted "unconstitutionally" under the Naturalist model (or under the Governmental model if a government official)? If not, then there is no *constitutional* grievance to assert in any court, state or federal, though there is still the state-provided damages remedy available in state court.

This difficulty in defining unconstitutional acts is part of the explanation why the area of "constitutional torts" by government officials has proved to be particularly vexing to courts and commentators. Regardless of which model is employed, some controversial boundaries must be established on the reach of constitutional suits; those boundaries will be conceptual, not substantive, in character. (Under the Legalist model, the "constitutional tort" problems lie in defining when an official's act is one of lawmaking in situations in which the act is neither expressly forbidden nor expressly authorized; and, if the act is lawmaking, in determining whether the act is unconstitutional given the actor's subjective perspective.)[3]

6

Three Hybrid Models

Now that we have articulated the three basic, concentric models for the Constitution's referent and have explored their deficiencies, we turn briefly to a project spawned of a desire for analytical completeness. Three additional, nonconcentric models may be posited in answer to the question of whom the Constitution commands.

These three models are produced by hybridizing the pure models we have described above. Each of them accords with the following analytical patterns:

> First, combine the referent of a relatively restrictive model with the referent of a relatively expansive model. For example, combine the referent of the Legalist model (lawmakers only) with the referent of the Naturalist model (everyone). Then:
>
> Whenever the legal regime in question is not unconstitutional, the dictates of the more limited model pertain.
>
> Whenever the legal regime in question is unconstitutional, the dictates of the more expanded model pertain.

It follows that no hybrid model is needed to explain the result of any particular case: in terms of results, the case can be explained in terms either of the more restrictive model or of the more expansive model. The analytical value of the hybrid models is found in attempts to explain the language used by a court in reaching a particular result, and frequently also in attempts to explain a group of cases that, taken together, seem to follow no particular pure model.

THE LEGALIST/NATURALIST MODEL

According to the Legalist model, lawmaking officials are the only constitutional-duty bearers, and defects in a legal regime are always material when called into question. According to the Naturalist model, everyone is a constitutional-duty bearer; and the presence of a defect-free legal regime, if an otherwise constitutionally inappropriate act is alleged, is not a material factor.

Now consider the situation in which the legal regime in question is alleged to contain a constitutionally defective law that, in turn, is *followed* by an actor against whom a constitutional claim is asserted. For example, consider a legal regime that confers a privilege on actors to infringe on some constitutionally protected interest of others. The actor infringes; his victim brings suit against him, asserting a constitutional violation by the actor.

The thoroughgoing Naturalist has no difficulty in accepting this assertion on its own terms: The actor was under a constitutional duty not to infringe, and has engaged in a constitutional violation without regard to whether the legal regime permitted the infringement. The Legalist, however, cannot accept the victim's assertion: The actor (if not a lawmaker acting in his capacity as a lawmaker) cannot be deemed to have breached a duty imposed upon him by the Constitution; any constitutional violation took place in the establishment of the legal regime under which the act took place; and the legal regime is not the direct target of the victim's suit. In short, we have a dispute, between the Naturalist model and the Legalist model, over how the victim's claim is to be conceptualized in terms of constitutional violation (or its absence) by the actor.

This dispute between Legalist and Naturalist may be compromised by the construction of a hybrid model, whose methodology proceeds as follows:

1. The Constitution imposes duties on lawmaking officials to enact constitutional laws (the Legalist model).

2. The Constitution imposes duties on all other persons—nonlawmaking officials and private citizens—to refrain from complying with unconstitutional laws (that is, laws that represent breaches of constitutional duties by lawmaking officials).

3. In the event of compliance with an unconstitutional law, the actor in compliance has breached a constitutional duty.

Perhaps our linguistic articulation of the Legalist/Naturalist model is enhanced by the representation of the model shown in Diagram 6.1 (to be compared with Diagrams 2.1 and 3.1).

Possibly *Lugar v. Edmundson Oil Co.* (1982)[1] furnishes an exemplar for the Legalist/Naturalist hybrid model. In *Lugar* the Supreme Court upheld as proper a federal section 1983 suit by a debtor brought against a private

DIAGRAM 6.1
THE LEGALIST/NATURALIST HYBRID MODEL I

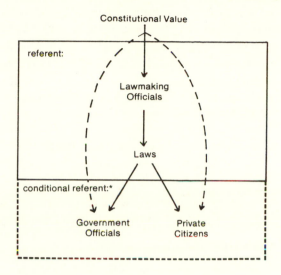

* that is: "in the event the laws are unconstitutional
that are made by lawmaking officials"

creditor who had acted in accordance with unconstitutional state attachment procedures. According to the Legalist/Naturalist, the creditor breached a constitutional duty, since the legal regime offended the Constitution, and the creditor acted in accordance with it. But just as possibly *Lugar* furnishes support for the Naturalist model, according to which the creditor's act was unconstitutional, whether or not in compliance with unconstitutional state law.[2]

THE LEGALIST/GOVERNMENTAL MODEL

A dispute between the Legalist and Governmental models, similar in form to that just identified between Legalist and Naturalist models, is present whenever a nonlawmaking government official is alleged to have breached a constitutional duty by acting in compliance with an unconstitutional law. Like the Naturalist, the Governmentalist would have no difficulties in conceptualizing the matter in such terms, while the Legalist would remain adamant that the government official has no constitutional duty to be breached.

This dispute between Legalist and Governmentalist is compromised in the following hybridized fashion:

1. The Constitution imposes duties on lawmaking officials to enact constitutional laws (the Legalist model).

2. The Constitution imposes duties on government officials (acting in their official capacity)—but not on private citizens—to refrain from complying with unconstitutional laws (that is, laws that represent breaches of constitutional duties by lawmaking officials).

3. In the event of compliance with an unconstitutional law while acting within the scope of official duty, the government official has breached a constitutional duty.

This model is shown in Diagram 6.2 (to be compared with Diagrams 2.1 and 4.1).

DIAGRAM 6.2
THE LEGALIST/GOVERNMENTAL HYBRID MODEL I

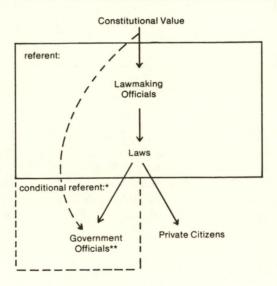

---

* that is: "in the event the laws are unconstitutional
  that are made by lawmaking officials"

** ... "acting in their official capacity"
  (otherwise, treated as "private citizens")

THE GOVERNMENTAL/NATURALIST MODEL

Finally, disputes between the Governmental and Naturalist models, arising when private citizens (or government officials acting outside their official capacities) harm constitutional values while acting in compliance with unconstitutional laws, may be compromised in the following hybridized fashion:

1. The Constitution imposes duties directly on all governmental officials who are acting in their official capacities, without regard to whether they are acting in compliance with other laws (the Governmental model).

2. The Constitution imposes duties on private citizens to refrain from complying with unconstitutional laws (that is, laws that represent breaches of constitutional duties by lawmaking officials) and with unconstitutional other acts by governmental officials.

3. In the event of compliance with an unconstitutional law (or other unconstitutional act of a government official), the private citizen has breached a constitutional duty.

This model is shown in Diagram 6.3 (to be compared with Diagrams 3.1 and 4.1).

CRITIQUE OF THE HYBRID MODELS

One's first impression is that these three hybrid models must be exemplars of those Calibans that sometimes are spawned in desperate intercourse between *a priori* and *ad hoc*, between abstract principles unfirmly held and heartfelt necessities of the particular case at hand.

None of these hybrids pretends to a principled foundation. Indeed, their respective rationales seem to be considerably weaker than those we have associated with the Governmental model; and, as we previously have shown, the Governmental model's principles derive solely from uneasy attempts to strike a compromise between the Legalist and Naturalist models. The thoroughgoing Legalist, of course, rejects all of these hybrids out of hand. The thoroughgoing Naturalist points gleefully to their presence, for they furnish good evidence of the Legalist model's difficulties whenever they are found in operation.

And the hybrid models are found in operation within the literature produced by our courts in grappling with the question of whom the Constitution commands. The Legalist/Naturalist, Legalist/Governmental, and Governmental/Naturalist models are not merely analytical poltergeists that rattle attempts to achieve a formal exegetical completeness. Many

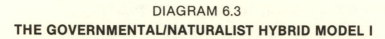

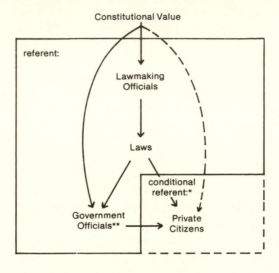

DIAGRAM 6.3

THE GOVERNMENTAL/NATURALIST HYBRID MODEL I

* that is: "in the event the laws, or other acts,
  are unconstitutional that are made by government officials"

** . . . "acting in their official capacity"
  (otherwise, treated as "private citizens")

Supreme Court decisions can at least be squared with one or another of the hybrid models, even if charity leads us to refuse to believe they have consciously been embraced.[3]

Perhaps, then, our first impressions are erroneous. Perhaps decent arguments can be made on their behalf. To this hypothesis we briefly turn.

Arguments for the Legalist Hybrids

Arguments for the Legalist hybrid models—the Legalist/Naturalist and Legalist/Governmental—proceed upon the view that it is superfluous to impose constitutional obligations on top of the nonconstitutional legal obligations that have been imposed by constitutionally proper laws. Thus the Legalist would maintain that obligations imposed by the Constitution are fully translated into, and exhausted by, the nonconstitutional legal obligations found in a constitutionally proper legal regime.

What is to be the position, then, when the nonconstitutional legal regime turns out to be constitutionally defective? The thoroughgoing Legalist has a ready answer to this question: The defective legal regime is subject to overthrow as violative of the Constitution's commands; but nonlawmaking acts, undertaken in pursuance of such a defective legal regime, are not within the compass of the Constitution's commands. Nevertheless, the suggestion is presented that, when the nonconstitutional legal regime is constitutionally defective, additional constitutional obligations are necessary to impose (upon an audience that is wider than the legal regime and its lawmakers) in order to secure constitutional values.

When this suggestion is embraced, the argument in support of one or the other Legalist hybrid model proceeds as follows:

> *The Legalist premise.* The Constitution imposes duties on lawmaking officials acting in their lawmaking capacities. If the law-makers fulfill those duties, then constitutional values are fully secured.

> *The conditional premise.* If the lawmakers breach their constitu-tional duties, they have not secured constitutional values. Constitu-tional values may nonetheless still be realized if the official (on the Legalist/Governmental model) or everyone (on the Legalist/Natur-alist model) ignores unconstitutional laws (and the unconstitutional absence of laws) and instead acts as though they were complying with a fully constitutional set of laws.

> *The conditional conclusion.* When the legal regime is unconstitu-tional, constitutional duties are to be imposed on persons (government officials, or everyone) in addition to lawmakers to act, contrary to the defective legal regime, in a "constitutional" manner.

A variant of this argument paradigm proceeds as follows. When the legal regime is constitutionally proper, the conscientious official and private citizen need look no further than to those nonconstitutional laws for the full measure of their legal duties. When the legal regime is constitutionally defective, however, we would like to hold officials and private citizens to legal duties that flow directly from constitutional values. These latter duties would require them to ignore constitutionally defective legal mandates, prohibitions, or permissions.

Thus we see the asymmetrical character of the Legalist hybrids: Each of them comports with the Legalist model when the laws in question are constitutional (hence no constitutional duties imposed on officials or private citizens). Each of them comports with another pure model (Governmental or Naturalist) when the laws in question are unconstitu-tional.

This asymmetry leads to easy response by proponents of either the pure Governmental or pure Naturalist model. The official (or citizen), in both the hybrid and the Governmental (or Naturalist) models, is required to look to the Constitution in order to assess whether a nonconstitutional law is constitutionally proper and thus legally obligatory. Therefore, it is fair to say that the official (or citizen) has violated a constitutional duty, not only whenever she follows an unconstitutional law (as the hybrid models hold), but also whenever she has violated a constitutionally proper law in a manner the Constitution could not permit to be legalized (as the pure Governmental or Naturalist model holds).

In any event, the argument paradigm we have sketched in support of the Legalist hybrid models is unconvincing on its own terms. It must assume that an official (or everyone) poses a greater threat to constitutional values when he acts in accordance with an unconstitutional set of laws than when he acts in violation of a constitutional set of laws. This assumption is incorrect, of course.

True, when a constitutionally permitted set of laws is violated, it is quite likely that a constitutionally adequate remedial law may apply with respect to the violation and its redress. Seldom, however, will the harm be completely reparable that is caused to the constitutional value by the violation.

Moreover, in most instances that can be imagined in which one would be tempted to press a Legalist hybrid model by virtue of its erroneous assumption, the model would not be necessary to apply in order to redress the violation. Suppose that an official (or citizen) acts in accordance with an unconstitutional set of laws and thus harms a constitutional value. That fact alone would not preclude the possibility that some other person—such as the victim of the violation, or governmental authorities—could then ignore those unconstitutional laws and act as though she were applying a constitutionally adequate remedial law in response to the wrongdoer's "legal" act.

In short, the Legalist hybrid models recognize the importance of the role that behavior beyond lawmaking plays in securing constitutional values. Whenever the argument is marshaled in support of the Legalist/Governmental model (behavior of government officials is a conditional constitutional target), the argument supports as well the invocation of the pure Governmental model. Whenever the argument is marshaled in support of the Legalist/Naturalist model (everyone's behavior is a conditional constitutional target), the argument supports as well the invocation of the pure Naturalist model.[4] (Indeed, this recognition—that behavior, not laws alone, is what ultimately is required in order to realize constitutional values—is one of the principal justifications for the adoption of a pure Naturalist model for the Constitution's referent.)

Despite the Legalist hybrid models' lack of cogency, there is case law that is consistent with these models, although it would be inaccurate to say that case law furnishes actual *support* for them. We have already mentioned *Lugar* as a case that is consistent with the Legalist/Naturalist model.[5] Then there are the many cases in which the plaintiff, alleging a constitutional violation, has brought suit seeking injunctive, declaratory, or damages relief against government officials who are acting in compliance with unconstitutional laws; these cases are consistent with the Legalist/Governmental hybrid model.[6]

We say that this case law is consistent with, but does not *support*, the Legalist hybrid models for several reasons. One reason is that there is case law that contradicts, as well as case law that is consistent with, each of the models we have described. The case survey in Appendix A discloses as much. Some of that case law must be incorrect—in any event, must not support—the Legalist hybrid models.

A second reason is that we need to know what "support" means in this context. Surely "support" does not mean "support as the exclusively appropriate model for the Constitution's referent." That is so because any case law that is consistent with a Legalist hybrid model necessarily is also consistent with the more extensive of the two pure models the hybrid attempts to combine. A case decision that "cannot be explained except by resort to the Legalist/Naturalist model," for example, is simply not so, because the same decision can be explained by resort to the pure Naturalist model. (Put differently, weak Legalists, not Naturalists, are the ones who need the explanations that lead to the Legalist/Naturalist—or Legalist/Governmental—hybrid models.)

The Governmental/Naturalist Hybrid Model

As with the Legalist hybrid models, the Governmental/Naturalist hybrid is nonconcentric and asymmetrical in character. As with the Legalist hybrid models, there are Supreme Court decisions that are consistent with, but that do not necessarily support, the Governmental/Naturalist model. The theory of the Governmental/Naturalist model is the same in form as the theory of the Legalist hybrid models, except that it commences with the Governmental model (which, recall, completely includes everything and everyone included in the Legalist model):

The Governmental Premise. The Constitution imposes duties on all government officials acting in their official capacities (including lawmaking officials acting in their lawmaking capacities). If the government officials fulfill those duties, then constitutional values are fully secured.

The conditional premise. If the government officials breach their constitutional duties, then they have not secured constitutional values. Constitutional values may nonetheless still be realized if private citizens ignore unconstitutional official acts (including unconstitutional laws) and the unconstitutional absence of official acts, and instead act as though they were complying with a fully constitutional set of official acts.

The conditional conclusion. When the acts of governmental officials are unconstitutional, constitutional duties are to be imposed on private citizens in addition to government officials to act, contrary to defective official acts, in a "constitutional" manner.

The Governmental/Naturalist model admits of one special critique when it is compared with the Legalist hybrid models. That critique rests on the pragmatic observation that the private citizen may find it considerably easier to fulfill her conditional constitutional duties by resisting or ignoring a lawmaker than by resisting a cadre of police officers armed with nightsticks, guns, and tear gas.

Otherwise, the arguments for and against the Governmental/Naturalist model are the combination of (1) the arguments for and against the Governmental model and (2) the arguments for and against the Legalist hybrid models, which we have previously discussed. In addition it should be noted that, since we find the Governmental model to be particularly problematic in its pure form,[7] we find the Governmental/Naturalist hybrid model to be so as well.

7

A Summary Description of the Six Models

For purposes of abstract summary description of the six models we have parsed, assume: Constitutional value CV mandates that lawmakers LM enact law L forbidding act A by official O and by private citizen PC. Then:

(1) *Legalist model (Diagram 2.1)*: If L is not enacted, LM has violated a constitutional duty, even if O and PC do not do A. If L is enacted, the Constitution is not violated, even if O and PC do A.

(2) *Governmental model (Diagram 4.1)*: LM's constitutional duty remains the same as in (1). In addition, O (while acting in O's official capacity), but not PC, has a constitutional duty not to do A, regardless of whether L is enacted.

(3) *Naturalist model (Diagram 3.1)*: LM's constitutional duty remains the same as in (1), and O's constitutional duty remains the same as in (2). In addition, PC has a constitutional duty not to do A, regardless of whether L is enacted or whether O is doing or not doing A.

(4) *Legalist/Governmental hybrid model (Diagram 6.2)*: LM's constitutional duty—to enact L—is the same as in (1). In addition, O (while acting in O's official capacity), but not PC, has a constitutional duty not to do A if L is not enacted. However, O has no constitutional duty (only a nonconstitutional duty) not to do A if L is enacted. Put differently, this model functions like the Legalist model when LM has enacted a constitutional set of laws, and like the Governmental model when LM has not done so.

(5) *Legalist/Naturalist hybrid model (Diagram 6.1)*: LM's constitutional duty—to enact L—is the same as in (1), and O's conditional

duty is the same as in (4). In addition, PC has a constitutional duty not to do A if L is not enacted. However, neither O nor PC has a constitutional duty (only a nonconstitutional duty) not to do A if L is enacted. Put differently, this model functions like the Legalist model when LM has enacted a constitutional set of laws, and like the Naturalist model when LM has not done so.

(6) *Governmental/Naturalist hybrid model (Diagram 6.3)*: LM's constitutional duty is the same as in (1), O's constitutional duty is the same as in (2), and PC's conditional constitutional duty is the same as in (5). In addition, PC has a conditional constitutional duty not to do A when L is not enacted and O orders PC to commit A. Put differently, this model functions like the Governmental model when LM has enacted a constitutional set of laws and O is fulfilling her constitutional duties, and like the Naturalist model when these conditions do not obtain.

Note again, to round out this summary, that the three pure models are concentric and symmetrical, while the three hybrid models are nonconcentric and asymmetrical. On the hybrid models, compliance with an unconstitutional legal regime has a different status from noncompliance with a constitutional legal regime; on the pure models, no such difference in status is admitted.

PART II _____

Implications of the Choice of Models

_____

Having described two basic models (the Legalist and Naturalist) for the Constitution's referent, together with the basic compromise model (the Governmental) and three hybrids derived from the three basic models, we now turn briefly to litigators' questions. Granted (we hope): As an academic exercise, it's nice to have models exposed that might serve to explain otherwise confused lines of cases. And given the academic exercise, the possibility is present that precedents may be reconciled or distinguished, for a purpose, by resort to these models.

But what is the cash value of the exegesis? What real differences—differences that translate into the decisionmaking processes we associate with litigation and adjudication—are to be identified in the survey of these models? What are the implications of choice, from among these models, with respect to the online litigation and adjudication of cases today and tomorrow in the state and federal courts?

We begin with the confession that, so far as concerns the work of the state courts, the main values of our exegesis are *conceptual, psychological,* and *terminological*:

> *conceptual,* because the models present perspectives about the relationships that are to be drawn among Constitution, "law," and the acts of alleged wrongdoers and their victims;

> *psychological,* because some may believe that claims of "constitutional violation" carry greater freight in litigation than do claims of ordinary illegality;

> *terminological,* because the models present to the state-court litigator ways of telling her stories, ways of articulating his pleadings.

This same confession, in the main, applies with respect to litigation in the federal courts that relates to the explicit legal regime—statutes, administrative regulations, and the like—of the federal government. Within these two large domains, a firm choice of model with respect to any given constitutional provision may impart consistency of analysis of claim and defense; but we hypothesize that the choice will not be outcome-determinative of the substantive merits of any lawsuit.

There remains a large domain of litigation to which, we believe, our confession does not apply. At least that is so on the terms we have thus far unveiled with respect to these models for the Constitution's referent. The domain encompasses the territory of concurrent state court and federal court original jurisdiction. We hypothesize that within this domain the choice from among these models, with respect to any constitutional provision or perhaps with respect to the Constitution as a whole, may well be outcome-determinative of such issues as whom to sue, in which court system, with respect to what kind of remedy. Indeed, the choice of model partially defines the territorial boundaries of the domain we have described.

We have promised brevity here. Brevity takes the form, not of a general survey of the entire range of issues to which the choice from among models may apply, but rather of the somewhat extended development of what we consider to be the two main areas of implication: first, what may be termed the "procedural/remedial" implications of the models; second, the apparently "substantive" issue of "state action." In Chapter 10, we will conclude with a brief discussion of the prescriptive implications, if any, with which the models (and choice from among them) leave us.

8

Choice of Forum, Remedy, and Defendant

The primary cash value of the choice, from among the models of whom the Constitution commands, lies in the models' respective implications for choice of forum, remedy, and defendant. If an act giving rise to an injury is not a constitutional violation, then, in the absence of some nonconstitutional basis for federal court jurisdiction, the actor will not be subject to suit in federal court. On the other hand, if the act is a constitutional violation, then federal courts clearly have power (under Article III of the Constitution) to adjudicate a suit brought against the actor.[1] On some of our models, an act infringing a constitutional value will surely give rise to a constitutionally based grievance, but will not itself be a constitutional violation; on other models the same act, committed by the same actor, will be a constitutional violation. Hence the cash value that attends the choice of models.

TWO MASTER HYPOTHETICALS

We will illustrate the implications for the choice of forum, remedy, and defendant of the various models by reference to two master hypotheticals. On entering, assume that it is unconstitutional for a state to permit creditor repossessions of household goods without some prior hearing on the alleged default.[2] Then:

> *Hypothetical One.* The lawmaking officials (LM) have, contrary to the constitutional norm, provided for a system of repossession of household goods by creditors without a prior hearing. The creditor (C) must obtain a writ from a law-executing official; thereafter he may

proceed on his own to take the goods of the debtor (D). C in fact obtains the writ and then, with the assistance of C's friend, an on-duty official (say, a marshal), takes D's goods. (We will use "O" to designate any government official, other than a lawmaker, who at least arguably is acting within the scope of his or her official capacity.)

Hypothetical Two. LM have, by statute, prohibited prehearing repossessions by creditors, as the Constitution requires. However, C, enlisting the assistance of O, takes D's goods in violation of the statute.

We believe it is fair to stipulate that, in each of these two master hypotheticals, the acts of C and O have infringed a constitutional value, giving rise to a constitutionally based grievance by D. The stipulation here does not impact adversely on our inquiry. Our inquiry is whether, under which of these hypotheticals, the acts of C and/or O amounted to a *constitutional violation* in taking D's goods, for which remedy may be sought not only in state court but also in federal court. In order to answer our inquiry, we need our models and the choice they present.

We shall analyze the implications of our models for the two hypotheticals based on alternative assumptions about the effect of the choice of model upon the possible *culpability* of officials and private citizens.

> The first analysis will assume that the choice of model does not affect the culpability of anyone. On this assumption, the determination of culpability is a product of actual conduct, the conduct's effect on constitutional values, and the actor's state of mind, and *not* a product of the abstract characterization of such conduct as a "constitutional violation."

> The second analysis will assume just the opposite: that whether one's conduct can be characterized as a constitutional violation will affect the determination of the actor's culpability and, in turn, the determination of potential liability for remedying constitutional violations.

It may be remarked that this split of analysis affects only Hypothetical One, in which the actors (C and O) act in pursuance of an unconstitutional set of laws. In Hypothetical Two, O and C are violators of *law* according to all models; thus, whether they are also violators of the Constitution seems superfluous, substantively speaking (albeit perhaps not psychologically speaking), to the determination of their culpability. But in Hypothetical One, in which actors C and O are complying with the nonconstitutional (and unconstitutional) "law," it is surely conceivable that their culpability (substantively speaking) may be affected by whether they are violating the

Constitution's commands in so acting or whether, instead, as the Legalist model has it, only the lawmaking officials are violating those commands. Ignorance that the law is unconstitutional, as opposed to ignorance of the law, may furnish excuse.

INTRODUCTION TO THE REMEDIAL META-REGIME

Having thus far defined our project here in terms of "constitutional violation" and "culpability," we now turn to the matter of *remedy*. Frequently, we think, questions of "constitutional violation" and "culpability" are conflated, in cases and commentary, with concerns that are associated with remedy. The conflation is a natural one, because a commonplace presumption is that "the person at fault (or most at fault) must pay." This maxim, while generally applicable and appropriate, does not always furnish an accurate description of the situation in litigation. Many occasions can be brought to mind—as when a wrongdoer possesses an immunity from determination of liability—in which those who are most culpable are subject neither to suit nor to liability. Many other occasions may be identified—regimes of vicarious liability, and perhaps of workers' compensation, furnish notable examples—in which remedy is exacted from relatively nonculpable parties.

Moreover, we believe it fair to assert that the Constitution does not operate monolithically with respect to type or timing of remedy for redress of constitutional violation. The actors we may deem to be most culpable may also, without offense to the Constitution, be appropriate targets only for particular remedies, incomplete remedies, or remedies that must be asserted in narrow time frames.

These noncontroversial considerations bring us to identify a theory—which we call the *remedial meta-regime*—that serves cogently to explain the constitutional relationship between constitutional violation, culpability, and remedy. The remedial meta-regime is the set of remedial laws that is mandated by constitutional values to deal with constitutional violations that harm those values.[3]

There are several important points to be made about the remedial meta-regime. First, the remedial meta-regime's prescriptions for whom to sue and for what remedy, given the occurrence of a constitutional violation, operate largely independently of the choice of model for whom the Constitution commands. The choice of model identifies who the constitutional violator or violators are. But the values that underlie the remedial meta-regime—the same constitutional values that underlie the Constitution's primary commands—may dictate in particular cases that (1) constitutional violators *are not* appropriate targets for constitutional remedies, and/or (2) others, not identified by the chosen model as constitutional violators, *are* appropriate targets for constitutional remedies.

Constitutional violators may not be appropriate targets for remedies under the remedial meta-regime in particular cases. That would be so either because constitutional values demand that those violators receive qualified or absolute immunity—as, for example, where the violators are lawmaking officials—or because the violators are sufficiently nonculpable that constitutional values preclude holding them liable (or holding them liable for certain remedies, such as consequential damages and/or punishment, as opposed to other remedies, such as injunction). Persons other than constitutional violators may be the appropriate targets for remedies under the remedial meta-regime in particular cases either because they are in fact culpable, or because the remedy is declaratory, injunctive, restitutionary, or otherwise works no serious hardship on them (and hence offends no constitutional values).

Indeed, it is accurate to say that if the choice of model does not affect the actual culpability of anyone—one of the two alternative assumptions about the relation between choice of model and culpability that we leave open—then the choice of model has absolutely no effect on the remedial meta-regime's selection of the appropriate defendants and remedies in suits based on constitutional violations.

The second important point to be made about the remedial meta-regime is that the remedial meta-regime may be implemented by the state courts, by the federal courts directly,[4] or by federal courts in pursuance of a federal statute enacted to implement the remedial meta-regime.[5] Therefore, the victim of a constitutional violation—in our master hypothetical above, D—may bring suit for redress of that harm in either federal or state court. D's choice between federal and state courts will be compelled only if Congress, with the permission of the remedial meta-regime, excludes federal court jurisdiction—or makes federal court jurisdiction exclusive—with respect to actions alleging harm to the constitutional value in question. If Congress has not thus dictated, then only if the remedial meta-regime permits alternative remedies and/or defendants—and then, only if Congress or the federal courts have chosen a different remedy/defendant from that chosen by the state courts—will D's choice of courts have any implications beyond forum and procedure.

The third important point to be made here, for our purposes, is that original federal court jurisdiction lies over *any* suit that invokes the constitutionally based remedial meta-regime. Such a suit is one "arising under" the Constitution regardless of whether the defendant is a constitutional violator.[6]

Although we maintain that the remedial meta-regime operates independently of the models for the Constitution's referent, its conceptualization differs somewhat depending on the model that is chosen. We present, in Diagrams 8.1-8.6, our conceptualization of the six models we have discussed previously, combined with their versions of the remedial meta-regime.

DIAGRAM 8.1
THE LEGALIST MODEL II

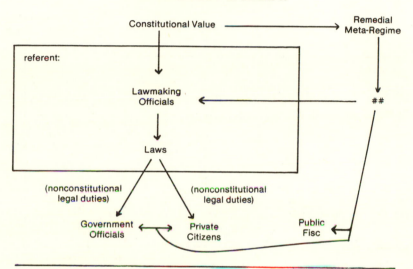

possible remedies if legal regime is
constitutionally defective

DIAGRAM 8.2
THE NATURALIST MODEL II

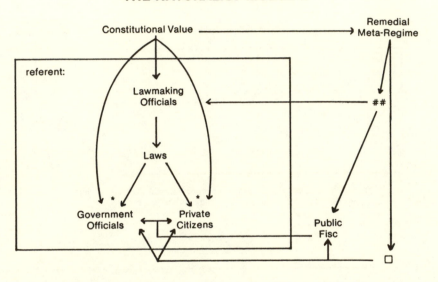

* constitutional as well as nonconstitutional
  duties with respect to the same acts

possible remedies if legal regime is
  constitutionally defective.

☐ possible remedies if legal regime is constitutionally
  proper but disobeyed.

DIAGRAM 8.3
THE GOVERNMENTAL MODEL II

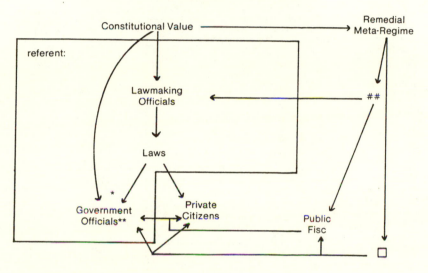

* constitutional as well as nonconstitutional
  duties with respect to the same acts

** ... "acting in their official capacity"
   (otherwise, treated as "private citizens")

possible remedies if legal regime is
   constitutionally defective

☐ possible remedies if legal regime is constitutional
  proper but disobeyed

DIAGRAM 8.4
THE LEGALIST/NATURALIST HYBRID MODEL II

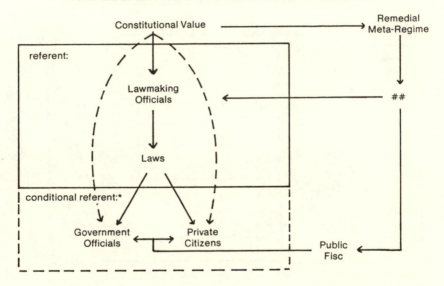

* that is: "in the event the laws are unconstitutional
  that are made by lawmaking officials"

possible remedies if legal regime is
  constitutionally defective

DIAGRAM 8.5
THE LEGALIST/GOVERNMENTAL HYBRID MODEL II

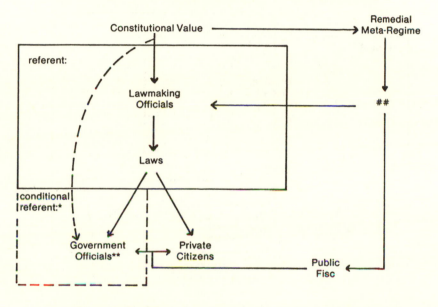

* that is: "in the event the laws are unconstitutional
  that are made by lawmaking officials"

** ... "acting in their official capacity"
   (otherwise, treated as "private citizens")

possible remedies if legal regime is
   constitutionally defective

DIAGRAM 8.6
THE GOVERNMENTAL/NATURALIST HYBRID MODEL II

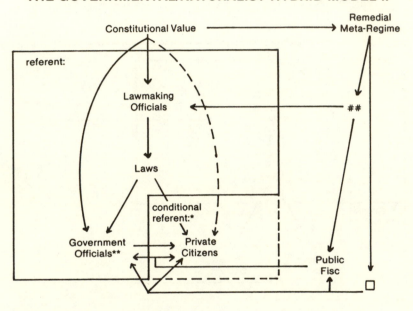

---

* that is: "in the event the laws, or other acts,
  are unconstitutional that are made by government officials"

** ... "acting in their official capacity"
  (otherwise, treated as "private citizens")

\#\# possible remedies if legal regime is
  constitutionally defective

☐ possible remedies if legal regime is constitutionally proper
  but is disobeyed by government officials

With this introduction of matters of pertinence—constitutional violation, culpability, and remedy—we turn to our two master hypotheticals and to the way our six models would suggest that they be treated in terms of choice of forum, remedy, and defendant.

HYPOTHETICAL ONE: THE UNCONSTITUTIONAL LEGAL REGIME

On the Legalist Model

The constitutional violation. D has been injured in a manner that a constitutionally valid set of state laws would prohibit and remedy. The injury is to a constitutional value. The constitutional violation, on the Legalist model, is simply that LM have unconstitutionally failed to enact the prohibition and attendant remedy. The result of that constitutional violation is that C and O have taken action, in accordance with an unconstitutional permission granted by LM, to deprive D of D's property.

Culpability. To us, LM seem clearly to be culpable. We did not need the Legalist model in order to arrive at our conclusion that LM are culpable. The culpability of LM remains the same to us, regardless of the model chosen for the Constitution's referent, so far as Hypothetical One is concerned.

The respective culpability of C and O seems roughly equivalent to us; but both the quality and the extent of their culpability is less clear, and in any event less than that of LM. Again, we do not think that we needed the Legalist model in order to arrive at this conclusion; our conclusion about *relative* culpability—as between LM on the one hand, C and O on the other hand—will remain the same regardless of the model chosen for the Constitution's referent. However, we do observe that on the Legalist model the culpability of C and O is either nonexistent (because they are guilty of neither constitutional violation nor violation of nonconstitutional laws) or unclear.

Remedy. The constitutional value at stake in Hypothetical One would undoubtedly mandate that the courts provide D with some sort of appropriate remedy (damages, restitution, declaration of the legal regime's unconstitutionality, and so forth). The remedial meta-regime would combine with that constitutional value (as qualified by other intersecting constitutional values) to identify which of the following were appropriate targets for which remedies: LM (the lawmaking officials);[7] C (the private party); O (the nonlawmaking officials); and/or the public fisc.[8]

On the Legalist model, only lawmakers are constitutional violators. The lawmakers may turn out to be immunized, either from any remedy imposed by any court directly upon them, or from particular remedies (such as damages) imposed by any court directly upon them, or from any (or particular) remedies imposed upon them by the federal courts as opposed to the state courts. This immunity, even in the context of Hypothetical One, may be granted by the Constitution itself, or by nonconstitutional laws that are deemed to be in accordance with the Constitution. Thus, it may turn out to be the case in Hypothetical One that LM are not subject to imposition of remedy, and hence are not fitting targets for suit, either in any court or in federal court.

Nevertheless, it does not follow on the Legalist model that no suit would lie against anyone if no suit lies against LM in Hypothetical One. Constitutionally mandated remedies—mandated by the remedial meta-regime—may nonetheless lie against private citizens, nonlawmaking officials, or the public fisc, depending on the circumstances in which constitutional values are harmed, on the litigation context presented to the court, and on the type of remedy sought by the victim of constitutional violation.

Moreover, D's action for remedy against C or O lies either in federal court or in state court, in the absence of an explicit, constitutionally permitted, and probably congressionally imposed limitation on the jurisdiction of either of these court systems. D's action lies in federal court because it properly invokes the Constitution-based remedial meta-regime in response to a constitutional violation, assuming that the remedy sought by D is mandated or permitted by the remedial meta-regime. D's suit is one "arising under" the Constitution.[9]

On the Three "Naturalist" Models

The constitutional violation. On the three "Naturalist" models—pure Naturalist, Legalist/Naturalist, and Governmental/Naturalist—every one of the actors has engaged in a constitutional violation. On the pure Naturalist model, LM, C, and O all have acted to infringe a constitutional value in a way that the Constitution prohibits; the acts of each of them create a constitutional violation by each. All actors have engaged in constitutional violations on the two Naturalist hybrid models as well: on those models the Constitution forbids acts by anyone that are in accordance with unconstitutional laws (but not acts that are violative of constitutional laws).

Culpability. If we assume that the choice of model does not affect our assessment of culpability, then our assessment of the culpability of the actor does not depend on whether the actor has committed a constitutional violation. Then, with respect to Hypothetical One, our assessment under the three "Naturalist" models of the respective culpability of the actors remains the same as on the Legalist model: LM clearly is culpable; C and O bear roughly equivalent culpability, which culpability is less in quality and extent than the culpability of LM.

If instead we assume that the choice of model does affect our assessment of culpability, then: (1) our assessment of LM's culpability remains constant on all models; (2) our assessment of the culpability of C and O is that these two actors have greater culpability on the three Naturalist models than they have on the Legalist model, although the question remains open whether their culpability now equals that of LM. On the three "Naturalist" models, everyone is under a constitutionally imposed obligation to refrain from acting in accordance with unconstitutional laws. All actors in Hypothetical One have breached this constitutionally imposed obligation, and hence have committed constitutional violations.

The value of the break in our analysis here between two contradictory assumptions about culpability is to be found primarily in the consequences that each analysis may have on choice of defendant(s) and remedies. Accordingly, this bifurcated analysis of culpability is carried into our discussion of "remedy" under the three "Naturalist" models.

Remedy. We believe that determinations of culpability have cash value, in litigation, primarily in terms of liability exposure: that is, in who is a candidate for the imposition of liability for what sort of remedy. Thus, if the determination of "constitutional violation" does not affect the determination of "culpability," then it follows that determination of "constitutional violation" likewise does not affect determination of liability. The contrary might be the case if determination of "constitutional violation" did affect determination of "culpability."

On the assumption that "commission by actor of constitutional violation" does not affect liability, the choice of defendants, remedies, and court is not affected by the selection of any of the three "Naturalist" models as opposed to the Legalist model. The fact that C and O—in addition to LM—are deemed to be constitutional violators on the "Naturalist" models does not make them more fitting candidates for defendant status, or more fitting targets for D's remedy, than they were on the Legalist model according to which they were not constitutional violators. Only the abstract conceptualization of their conduct—not the conduct itself, their states of mind, or other factors relevant to choice of remedy and its target—has changed. The remedial meta-regime will identify exactly the same defendant(s) and remedies as on the Legalist model; and both sets of courts, state and federal, will have jurisdiction to entertain D's suit.

On the assumption that "commission by actor of constitutional violation" does affect liability (as a result of affecting our determination of culpability), the choice of defendant(s) and remedies on the three "Naturalist" models may differ from the choice we make on the Legalist model. That is so because C and O are violators of constitutional commands, and thus have personal culpability, on the three "Naturalist" models but not on the Legalist model. In turn, their personal culpability will make them more fitting targets, on the "Naturalist" models and under the remedial meta-regime, for such remedies as consequential or punitive damages, and perhaps even criminal sanctions.

Again, however, the choice of court systems is unaffected, in theory at least, by the choice of one of the "Naturalist" models as opposed to the Legalist model: The constitutionally based remedial meta-regime continues to lie within the jurisdiction of either federal or state court (in the absence of explicit direction to the contrary); and each court system might choose, or might be required by the remedial meta-regime to impose, the identical remedies against the identical defendants regardless of the model chosen for the Constitution's referent.

So far as injunctive, declaratory, or restitutionary relief is concerned, we believe that the Legalist and three "Naturalist" models dictate the same remedies (against the same defendants) regardless of the assumption we make about culpability for constitutional violation in the context of Hypothetical One. With regard to other types of remedy—the more "punitive" forms—however, the choice of assumptions about culpability likely will lead to a divergence of available remedy between Legalist and "Naturalist" models. If the Legalist model is chosen, then regardless of the assumption about culpability that is chosen, the likely result would be that "punitive" remedies would be unavailable against C or O.

If one of the "Naturalist" models is chosen, and the assumption also is chosen that culpability is affected by constitutional violation, then "punitive" remedies against C and O would most likely be available. However, even then we would expect to see the development of a form of affirmative defense, available to C and O, that their acts in pursuance of an unconstitutional law excuse them from the imposition of "punitive" remedies; if not, then a strong case could be made out that they have a right of indemnity, assertable against the public fisc (if not also against LM), with respect to "punitive" remedies imposed upon them.

On the Two "Governmental" Models

The constitutional violation. On the two "Governmental" models—pure Governmental and Legalist/Governmental—LM and O, but not C, have engaged in constitutional violations in the context of Hypothetical One. On the pure Governmental model, LM and O all have acted to infringe a constitutional value in a way that the Constitution prohibits; the acts of each of them create a constitutional violation by each. On the Legalist/ Governmental hybrid model as well, these same actors—again, excluding private citizen C—have engaged in constitutional violations: on this model the Constitution forbids acts by government officials that are in accordance with unconstitutional laws (but not acts that are violative of constitutional laws).

Culpability. If we assume that the choice of model does not affect our assessment of culpability, then our assessment of the culpability under the two "Governmental" models in the context of Hypothetical One remains the same as on the Legalist model (LM clearly is culpable; O—and C as well—bear roughly equivalent culpability, which culpability is less in quality and extent than the culpability of LM). If instead we assume that the choice of model does affect our assessment of culpability, then the culpability of O—but not of C—is the same as on the three "Naturalist" models when the same assumption was made.

Remedy. The same analysis regarding liability, choice of defendants, remedy, choice of court, and possibility of affirmative defenses and/or indemnity applies here to O (but not to C) as we discussed in connection with the three "Naturalist" models. All that we think might bear repeating here is that, regardless of the model chosen for whom the Constitution commands, the presence of the constitutionally based remedial meta-regime means that D's suit for remedy—against whatever defendant(s), for whatever relief that might be entailed in the choice of model together with the assumption made regarding the impact of a determination of "constitutional violation" on assessment of culpability—continues to permit the choice of either a federal court or a state court for the forum in which the suit is presented, in the absence of explicit (probably congressional) direction to the contrary, so far as Hypothetical One is concerned.

Summary of the Application of the Models in Hypothetical One

The choice of model for the Constitution's referent *never* has implications regarding the question of whether someone has suffered a grievance that is premised on infringement of a constitutional value and that is traceable to an act that is illegal in some sense.

If we assume that the choice of model does *not* affect our assessment of culpability, then in Hypothetical One, where LM has enacted an unconstitutional set of laws dealing with creditor repossession, the choice among the models of whom the Constitution commands has absolutely no implications regarding the questions of whom to sue, which court (state or federal) to select, and what remedy to seek.

The remedial meta-regime may permit some alternatives in terms of choice of defendant and of remedy. If so, then the defendant/remedy choices of the federal courts (if unaided by statute) might differ from the defendant/remedy choices of the various state court regimes in implementing the remedial meta-regime; and both federal court and state court choices in this regard might conceivably differ from Congress' choice of defendant/remedy in implementing the remedial meta-regime. These choices, however, will be totally unaffected by the choice from among our models if the assumption is that choice of model does not affect assessment of culpability.

If we assume that the choice of model does affect our assessment of culpability, then the choice of model may indeed have implications for the choice of defendant and remedy. On the Naturalist, Legalist/Naturalist, and Governmental/Naturalist models, C and O are more culpable than they are on the Legalist model—hence more eligible, perhaps, for liability and for a wider range of remedies—under the remedial meta-regime. On the Governmental and Legalist/Governmental models, O (but not C) is a more eligible candidate for liability and range of remedy than he is under the Legalist model. The remedial meta-regime, however, might well dictate the provision of affirmative defense, or indemnity from the public fisc, for any liability that these additionally culpable actors incur beyond restitution, given that they acted in accordance with the state's "laws."

Our analysis of Hypothetical One can help to clarify difficult section 1983 cases. *Lugar v. Edmundson Oil Co.* (1982),[10] for example, is factually identical to Hypothetical One. Section 1983—the statute at issue in *Lugar*—can be considered as a means chosen by Congress to implement the remedial meta-regime. Thus:

When LM have enacted unconstitutional laws, and injury to a constitutional value either has occurred or imminently is threatened, the time for resort to remedies prescribed by the remedial meta-regime is ripe on all the models. Section 1983 authorizes a remedy against those who effect such an injury "under color of law," which could be construed as follows: "When the laws are unconstitutional, and injury is threatened or has occurred, pick the legal and/or equitable remedy, together with the defendant(s), that are most appropriate for preserving the values of the Constitution."[11]

In cases like *Lugar* (or Hypothetical One), creditor C, who is acting in pursuance of unconstitutional attachment laws, seems to be the appropriate target for a restitutionary suit. If we assume that the choice of model does not affect culpability, then C does not seem to be an appropriate target for consequential damages, given the average C's ignorance of constitutional law and the threat to other constitutional values that is entailed in strict liability for acting in pursuance of unconstitutional laws. The appropriate target for consequential damages on this assumption is probably the public fisc, not O, whose acts are probably no more culpable than the acts of C, and not LM, whose acts (even if culpable) are probably best left immunized from liability in order to preserve other constitutional values. (If proper construction of section 1983[12] or of the Eleventh Amendment does not permit the provision of a *federal* remedy against the state's public fisc, then D would have to resort to the *state* courts for recovery of these consequential damages.)[13]

If, on the other hand, we assume that the choice of model does affect culpability, then C and O on the three "Naturalist" models (and O but not C on the two "Governmental" models) *are* appropriate targets for the full range of remedies (such as consequential damages, as in *Lugar*),[14] although they in turn might have a right of indemnity against the public fisc.

Our analysis also places Eleventh Amendment cases like *Ex Parte Young* (1908)[15] on a more secure analytical footing. In allowing injunctions against state officials who enforce laws that are violative of the Fourteenth Amendment, the *Young* court failed to explain satisfactorily how it was that the official represented "the state" for purposes of the state action requirement but nonetheless did not represent "the state" for purposes of the Eleventh Amendment. On our analysis, however, the solution to *Ex Parte Young's* conundrum is straightforward.

The analysis is this: On all models for whom the Constitution commands, the state's lawmakers, in enacting an unconstitutional law, have acted unconstitutionally under the Fourteenth Amendment. The remedy prescribed by the remedial meta-regime—prior to enforcement of the unconstitutional law—is an injunction directed at the enforcing official. Such an injunction is an appropriate remedy because the constitutional values that are of concern to the Eleventh Amendment are not threatened by injunctions against unconstitutional laws, even when actions for injunctions are brought in the federal courts.[16]

HYPOTHETICAL TWO: THE CONSTITUTIONALLY PROPER LEGAL REGIME

In Hypothetical Two, the state's LM have properly forbidden prehearing repossessions; but C, with the aid of O, has violated state law and repossessed before allowing D a hearing.

On the Three "Legalist" Models

The constitutional violation. On the three "Legalist" models—the pure Legalist, Legalist/Naturalist, and Legalist/Governmental—no one has violated any constitutional command. Hence no constitutional violation is present.

Culpability. Surely we have culpable actors—C and O—on our hands. Their culpability, however, is not predicated on any constitutional violation, according to the three "Legalist" models.

Remedy. The remedial meta-regime has no unconstitutional act to which to respond. Hypothetical Two, on the "Legalist" models, presents no constitutional case; and the federal courts lack jurisdiction, if there is no nonconstitutional predicate for such jurisdiction, to entertain any suit brought by D against C and O.

Of course, there has been a violation of state law in Hypothetical Two, and that violation has resulted in an injury to D that implicates a constitutional value. State law remedies are present, however, to be invoked against C and O; and, by hypothesis, those state remedies are constitutionally adequate to rectify the harm to the constitutional value in question. If D wants a remedy for the injury suffered, then—despite the presence of harm to a constitutional value—D's only recourse is to those state remedies on the three "Legalist" models.

On the Naturalist Model

The constitutional violation. The presence of constitutionally proper laws, on the Naturalist model, does not save C and O from being constitutional violators in addition to being state law violators. D has been the victim of unconstitutional acts (the acts of C and O).

Culpability. The culpability of C and O is established by their violation of state law. As we have indicated previously, the presence of "constitutional violation" is superfluous for assessment of culpability under Hypothetical Two.

Remedy. The remedial meta-regime is implicated, on the Naturalist model, by the acts of C and O. D's suit against them can be deemed to be a case "arising under" the Constitution; accordingly, the federal as well as the state courts have constitutionally based jurisdiction over the suit. (No reasonable construction of the "under color of law . . ." language of section 1983—within the narrow terms of Hypothetical Two—would confer federal court jurisdiction over D's suit against C, as opposed to D's suit against O. D's suit against C, if brought in federal court, would have to be a "*Bivens* action" brought directly under the Constitution.)[17]

Of course, on the Naturalist model—as on all models—D is free to bring suit against C and O in state court on claims asserting a constitutional violation. In Hypothetical Two, D could sue C and O on either, or both, a constitutional cause of action or a state law cause of action. And here is what's interesting:

> The remedy and choice of defendants that is identified by the remedial meta-regime in response to the constitutional violation will be exactly the same remedy/defendant that state law identifies as its response to the state law violation. Or, if the remedial meta-regime identifies alternative remedies/defendants, then the state laws will include at least one of those alternatives.

C and O have violated the Constitution on the Naturalist model. The constitutionally based remedial meta-regime prescribes the remedy or remedies for their constitutional violation. But (in Hypothetical Two) because the state's laws, *including its remedial laws,* are constitutionally adequate, the state remedial laws applicable to C and O must either be mandated by the remedial meta-regime or be among the alternatives thus mandated.

The approach of the state courts to the constitutional cause of action will be no different from their approach to the state law cause of action. The approach of the federal courts to the constitutional cause of action *may* be the same as the approach of the state courts, if the federal courts choose the same remedy/defendant option that the state law has chosen from the options permitted by the remedial meta-regime, and *will* be the same if the remedial meta-regime prescribes only one remedy/defendant choice.

On the Two "Governmental" Models

The constitutional violation. On the two "Governmental" models—the pure Governmental and the Governmental/Naturalist hybrid model—D has been the victim of an unconstitutional act. That unconstitutional act—the constitutional violation—is the act of O (but not of C). If O had not accompanied C in the repossession of D's goods, then the two "Governmental" models would operate in exactly the same manner as would the three "Legalist" models, and D would have only a state law cause of action against C on all five of these models.

Culpability. The culpability of O (but not of C) would be embellished by the addition of "constitutional violation" to state law violation, according to the two "Governmental" models. Previously we have posited, however, that any embellishment in this regard would be substantively (though perhaps not psychologically) superfluous so far as determination of culpability is concerned.

Remedy. Given O's acts in Hypothetical Two, the two "Governmental" models operate in exactly the same manner, with regard to choice of court, choice of defendant, and remedy, as does the Naturalist model.

It may be that the remedial meta-regime mandates that any remedy be directed against C but not against O; or it may be that the remedial meta-regime permits the immunization of O from liability, under the circumstances of Hypothetical Two. In such an event, suit would lie only against C. That suit, however, would lie within the jurisdiction of either federal or state court, on both state and federal-constitutional causes of action—even though, on the Governmental model, the constitutional violation was O's act, not C's. As in our discussion of Hypothetical One, it is the presence of

the constitutional violation—not the constitutional violator or defendant—
that invokes the remedial meta-regime; and, once it is properly invoked,
federal court jurisdiction is implicated in the absence of an explicit
(probably congressional) direction to the contrary.

Summary of the Application of the Models in Hypothetical Two

The practical difference—the *only* practical difference—between the
Legalist and Legalist hybrid models on the one hand, and the pure
Naturalist model on the other hand, boils down to this:

> When the state laws are constitutional but have been violated in a
> manner that could not constitutionally be permitted—our Hypothetical
> Two—the Naturalist model permits a suit in federal court, and the
> three Legalist models do not permit a suit in federal court.

> The Naturalist's suit in federal court *may* lie against a different
> defendant, and *may* seek a different remedy, from the defendant sued
> and remedy sought by the Naturalist in state court—depending on
> whether the remedial meta-regime prescribes alternative remedy/
> defendant options.

The Governmental model and Governmental/Naturalist hybrid model are
applied, in Hypothetical Two, like the three "Legalist" models when no
official has violated the constitutionally mandated state laws; they are
applied like the Naturalist model when an official has violated those laws.

9

"State Action" and the Substantive Merits

Everyone moderately fluent in constitutional law is familiar with the "state action" issue that arises in litigation under the Fourteenth and Fifteenth Amendments and several of the first ten amendments. A person challenges the action of another person as depriving the former of some constitutional right. The latter replies that she is not the government, that the constitutional right in question is a right against the government not private persons, and that therefore the challenge is unmeritorious. The Supreme Court's resolutions of such cases are egregiously confusing and unprincipled, even to those who find most of the Court's work product confusing and unprincipled.[1]

One of us wrote several years ago that the Court's handling of the state action issue was confusing and unprincipled because there really was not a state action issue.[2] Proper conceptual analysis would reveal that the state action issue was bogus; the belief that there was such an issue deflected attention away from the real issues that lurked behind the nonissue of state action. Confusing and unprincipled outcomes were to be expected so long as this attention to a nonissue and failure to attend to real issues persisted.

That position was a half-truth. If the state action issue is really another name for the question of whom the Constitution commands—the choice among the three models we have identified and their three hybrid variants—then there *is* a real and important state action issue. If, however, the state action issue is regarded as germane to the ultimate merits underlying a constitutional claim—whether a person has been deprived of an entitlement traceable to the Constitution—then the state action issue is bogus.

As we have shown, the choice among the models for the Constitution's referent will perhaps sometimes determine who should be sued, for what remedy, and in what court, and whether the claim is a constitutional claim or merely a state (or federal nonconstitutional) law claim that is supported by the Constitution. (As we also have shown, the differences in these regards that are produced upon analysis of these models turn out to be less than might have been imagined.) But the choice among models will not determine who should ultimately prevail on the substantive claim over whether a legal right of some sort has been violated.

This point can be illustrated by comparing the two extreme models—the Legalist (most restrictive, least inclusive) and Naturalist (least restrictive, most inclusive) models—for answering the question of whom the Constitution commands.

The Legalist model directs us to ask whether the laws of the state are the laws permitted or required by the Constitution. But every act that might aggrieve another, whether taken by a government official or private citizen, has a legal status under the laws of the state: The act is either required, permitted, or forbidden; and, if the latter, then it is subject to varying degrees of legal redress.[3] For this reason, every grievance for which the laws of the state give no redress can be translated into a grievance about those laws of the state and their failure to give redress, and thence can be translated into a constitutional grievance.

Thus, suppose constitutional value CV requires a state to have both (1) a law forbidding private citizens from engaging in conduct M and (2) a law granting a cause of action for damages and other remedies to persons who are injured by persons who engage in conduct M. Suppose further that a state has no such laws, and that a person is injured by another person's conduct M.

The injured person will have a constitutional grievance: one against the lawmakers on the Legalist model; or one against the injurer as well as the lawmakers on the Naturalist model. The choice of model could dictate the injured party's choice of court and perhaps her choice of defendant, but it will not affect the merits of her claim.

Likewise, if instead the state had in force all of the CV-mandated laws, the injured person would still have a constitutional grievance against her injurer on the Naturalist model. And although she would have no *constitutional* grievance against anyone on the Legalist model—because on that model the Constitution commands only lawmakers, who by hypothesis have fulfilled their constitutional duties—she would nonethless have her *state law* grievance against her injurer. Moreover, it seems logical to assume that the proper remedy or alternative remedies for the constitutional grievance on the Naturalist model would be the identical remedy or alternative remedies that on the Legalist model the state is compelled to provide for the state law claim.

Thus, whatever the model, the injured person may have the same grievance against the same defendant for the same remedy. The only possible difference separating the two extreme models would lie in choice of court (federal versus state) and label (''constitutional violation'' versus ''state law violation'') for the grievance.[4]

The absence of any ''state action'' problem does not mean, however, that the cases are not problematical that are thought of as ''state action'' cases. Most of them are problematical, not because of the lack of state action, but rather because the state action involved is difficult to assess in terms of the constitutional merits. We illustrate this point by assuming that the most restrictive (Legalist) model is thought to govern.

Four types of state action can be distinguished: (1) laws governing proprietary action by government; (2) prohibitory laws directed at private citizens; (3) permissive laws directed at private citizens (the ''hole'' of legally permitted private action surrounded by the ''doughnut'' of prohibitory state action); and (4) permissive laws joined with state aid in connection with the permission. The first two categories have raised no ''state action'' problems for the courts, while the last two have. The reason is not that the last two are not state action: they must be, because the legal regime is ''state action'' on all models, permissions are aspects of the regime, and permissions are effectuated through prohibitory state laws that are clearly state action.[5] The reason for the courts' difficulties is that permissive laws may have legitimate governmental interests in support of them—such as protecting individual privacy, autonomy, and belief—that are lacking in analogous proprietary and prohibitory state action.[6]

One example in the permissive law category is the famous case of *Shelley v. Kraemer* (1948),[7] which involved the law of covenants. That law permitted a broad range of private agreements, including agreements not to sell to blacks. Like all permissive laws, it was buttressed by prohibitory laws—those requiring convenantors to abide by their agreements and requiring third persons to observe the property rights that were established through covenants.

Shelley, which deemed the Missouri courts' enforcement of racially restrictive covenants to be unconstitutional state action, is an unsettling case for most commentators, because it implies by its analysis that it is unconstitutional for the state to enforce any private discriminatory acts that the state itself could not constitutionally undertake. Thus, goes the *reductio* of *Shelley*, having the police or courts assist those who practice racial discrimination in inviting guests to dinner at their houses would be unconstitutional state action. The *reductio* simply cannot be correct. *Shelley* must therefore be wrong.

The problem is that *Shelley* is *not* wrong in holding that judicial enforcement of covenants is state action. (Whether one includes permissive laws within state action, or restricts state action to the prohibitory laws that complement all permissive laws, is irrelevant. So, too, is the question of whether courts make law or apply preexisting law. In either case, *some* Missouri institution has made the law in question.) Indeed, the Court continues to follow this aspect of the *Shelley* holding.[8] Nor was *Shelley* wrong in acknowledging that state-mandated neighborhood segregation was unconstitutional action. (The Supreme Court had previously so held in *Buchanan v. Warley* [1917].)[9]

Instead, the problem in *Shelley* was in assuming that its conclusion—that Missouri's action was unconstitutional state action—followed without more from its two premises: (1) judicial enforcement of restrictive convenants is state action; and (2) state-imposed racial segregation of neighborhoods is unconstitutional. What was needed in *Shelley* was an argument that "the state action of judicial enforcement of private racial zoning through the enforcement of a race-neutral law of covenants" is constitutionally no more justifiable than the state action of state-mandated racial zoning.[10] That argument was never made because—although the Court glimpsed the truth that the state, through its laws, is involved in all action by virtue of its giving some legal status to all actions—it nevertheless failed to see that state involvement comes in relevantly different kinds.[11]

On the other hand, there are instances in which the government has less weighty, or at least no weightier, reasons for permitting private activity than it has for analogous action of its own. In those instances the courts' failure to recognize that, even on the maximally restrictive Legalist model, the laws of the state are clearly "state action" and are implicated in a constitutional claim can produce perverse decisions.

Suppose one were to object to the position that we have adopted, namely, that legal permissions are a form of state action. It is difficult to imagine why one would wish to do so on conceptual grounds alone, so let us assume that the objection is substantive. That is, the framers did not intend for legal permissions to be subjected to constitutional review in the light of constitutional values. There are several problems with such a position.

First, except in a condition of total anarchy, every legal permission takes place against a background of complementary legal prohibitions. The background prohibitions, of course, are paradigmatic "state actions." Thus, the legal permission to determine who enters one's house is complemented by the legal prohibition of trespass. It makes no substantive sense, much less conceptual sense, to deny review of the permission if the complementary prohibition can be reviewed. To say, for example, that the permission in *Shelley* to covenant to discriminate *is not* state action, but that the enforcement of the covenant—through prohibitions of the black purchasers' or white sellers' actions inconsistent with the covenant's terms—*is* state action, is either to assert a distinction without a difference, or is instead to place an unjustifiable weight on the posture or timing of legal proceedings rather than on their substance.

There is no reason, for example, to force blacks who wish to challenge the constitutionality of a state's permission of racial discrimination in the leasing of real property to employ self-help and occupy the property that has been denied them on racial grounds, and then raise their constitutional claim as a challenge to the state's prohibitory trespass law when it is applied to them. Indeed, because self-help of that type is socially undesirable, there is every reason to allow a constitutional suit directly challenging the permission that is backed by the prohibition. (We assume that no one wishes to take the quite radical position that the Constitution is unconcerned with privately enforced prohibitory laws, that is, private causes of action. Such a position would require rejecting, for example, all the decisions applying the First Amendment to defamation law in civil actions.)[12]

Second, although most state permissions may be substantively justified, even where analogous state proprietary actions—or state laws making mandatory that which is presently permitted—would be unconstitutional, some state permissions are undoubtedly substantively as bad or worse than analogous state proprietary actions or mandatory laws. A law "permitting" A to take others' property without compensation is an unconstitutional law, we submit, even though it is permissive only.[13] So, too, is a law that permits parents to assault or sexually abuse their children or each other.[14] Indeed, the Supreme Court in *Marsh v. Alabama* (1946)[15] found the permission to a private landowner to evict leafleteers to be unconstitutional, although the challenge in that case rose in the context of the complementary prohibition of trespass.[16]

Take the issue of repossession of goods prior to a full hearing on default. A legal regime that allows self-help repossession is, if anything, less likely to be in compliance with constitutional norms than is a legal regime that requires that repossession can be effected with the supervision of an official. That is, whether the state is acting through officials or is merely permitting private repossession is irrelevant to both the existence and the legitimacy of "state action": in either case there is state action in the form of the laws governing repossessions; and the laws allowing and giving legal effect to self-help repossession are, if anything, more constitutionally dubious than the laws authorizing state-assisted repossession.[17]

Nevertheless, while the Supreme Court has rather consistently struck down state laws authorizing state-assisted repossession,[18] it has upheld the validity of self-help repossession on the indefensible ground of "no state action."[19] Inexplicably, it has had no difficulty in finding "state action" behind a writ of garnishment,[20] although it could find no "state action" in the statutory grant of power to convey good title through sale by a bailee of a bailor's goods.[21]

One might posit a theory for "state action" that evinced substantive constitutional concern with only those permissions to private citizens that were coupled with some sort of monopoly power.[22] Such a theory would perhaps fare better than a theory that held all permissive laws to be beyond constitutional review. One who held such a theory might argue that the framers of the Constitution were concerned with abuses by those with whom citizens were forced to deal by virtue of possessing a *de jure* or *de facto* monopoly, usually the government, but sometimes private persons or enterprises as well.[23]

Such a theory could account for the Court's decision in *Marsh*. Perhaps it could also account for our intuitions regarding laws, like those we previously hypothesized, that give one private citizen legal permission to take others' property, or that give parents legal permission to abuse their children. Indeed, it might even justify the result in *Shelley v. Kraemer*.

We allude to this "monopoly power" theory in order to reiterate the level on which our exposition functions in this book. We observe that such a "monopoly power" theory for "state action" and state permissions to private citizens is not inconsistent with any position we have been taking. Such a theory, even if it proves to be correct, concedes that permissive laws may at times offend constitutional values; its concern is with what the substantive interpretation of those values may be. The only substantive position we have taken in this book is that permissive laws, in some situations (which we have not specified), may violate the Constitution.

On some other field of play we might be found to argue about whether "monopoly power" is the proper or complete theory for identifying which permissive laws amount to "unconstitutional state action."[24] The only point worth making here, however, is that a "monopoly power" theory—or any other theory designed to identify a substantive interpretation for "unconstitutional permissive state laws"—is entirely compatible with the substantive position we have taken here concerning "state action."

We are not denying that there is a distinction between legally supported private decisionmaking and decisionmaking by the government itself. That distinction of course exists, and it quite often can be a constitutionally significant distinction. Private decisionmakers have many reasons for decisions that justify legal support of those decisions—for example, autonomy, privacy, and religious beliefs—but that government cannot invoke to justify *its* decisions. What we are claiming is simply that: (1) the legal enforcement of private decisionmaking is an aspect of a state's legal regime, which, like any other aspect of the legal regime, can be assessed on its substantive constitutional merits; and (2) the legal enforcement of private decisionmaking is not always constitutional on its merits (as repossession, parental child abuse, and other examples indicate).[25]

Moreover, we are not quarreling here with the Supreme Court's seminal decision in the *Civil Rights Cases* (1883).[26] That decision can be read in two ways, both consistent with our position. First, the decision can be read as one on the merits—upholding the constitutionality of a legal regime that gives legal sanction to private decisionmaking that includes racial discrimination in public accommodations. Alternatively, the decision can be read as one adopting the Legalist model of whom the Constitution commands. On the latter analysis, the problem in the case was that the federal suit failed to allege that the lawmakers had violated the Constitution; instead, the suit focused merely on the acts of private defendants, who on the Legalist model cannot violate the Constitution.[27]

Of course, one would be free to quarrel with the *Civil Rights Cases* over whether the Legalist model is the appropriate one to adopt for the Constitution's referent. As we have shown, both in Chapter 2 and in Appendix A, the Supreme Court itself has quarreled with the *Civil Rights Cases,* on this level of discussion, in numerous later cases. Our purpose has not been to join in this quarrel, but rather to set forth the exegesis of the framework for such a quarrel, and then illustrate what the framework brings to bear on the likes of "state action doctrine."

Our conclusion is that there is no "state action" issue that affects the question of whether anyone has a legally meritorious claim that is connected with constitutional values. The only true "state action" issue is the issue of which of the models should be chosen that we have identified.[28] And, in turn, the choice from among our models does not affect the question of whether a claim is meritorious that alleges the infringement of constitutional values.[29]

10

The Choice among Models: Its Implications Summarized

In terms of their description, there are vast differences among the models that we have identified for whom the Constitution commands. Surprisingly, however, the prescriptive implications that attend the choice among these models appear to be almost evanescent.

The choice of model has no implications for deciding the substantive merits of claims that conduct has occurred that is proscribed by some legal regime (nonconstitutional or constitutional) and the proscription of which is mandated by constitutional values.

The only practical implication attending the choice of model is this: When the relevant nonconstitutional laws are constitutionally proper and have been violated (in a manner that the Constitution would not permit), the Legalist model and the two Legalist hybrids deny that a constitutional violation has occurred (and thus require resort to state law remedies, frequently only in state court), while the other three models affirm a constitutional violation and permit resort to federal court for constitutional remedies.

Even this practical difference among the models is diminished by the recognition that the constitutional remedies in federal court may very well be the identical remedies that are prescribed by state law and by virtue of which the state law is deemed to be constitutionally proper.

Where unconstitutional laws have been enacted (and have caused or threaten injury in their application), then, if we assume that the choice does not affect real-world culpability, the choice from among the available models has absolutely no implications for who can be sued, for what remedy, and in what court. (On this assumption, the Legalist hybrid models, which diverge from the Legalist model *only* when unconstitutional laws have been enacted, have absolutely no practical implications that differ from those of the Legalist model.) Only if we assume that the choice from among models actually does affect the determination of culpability will that choice affect who is to be sued for what remedy; but the choice of model still will not affect the choice of court, because a federal action (as well as a state action) under the remedial meta-regime remains available even on the pure Legalist model.

Given the very limited practical differences among the models, has it turned out that we have labored mightily to bring forth a mouse? Obviously, we do not think so; and here's why:

First, large numbers of cases involve situations in which the state laws are constitutionally proper but someone—almost always a government official, according to the extant case law that is pertinent to our discussion—has violated those laws in a manner that implicates constitutional values, and in which the plaintiff seeks to bring her claim in the federal courts on constitutional grounds. The usual question in these cases is whether the plaintiff has pleaded a constitutional cause of action (over which the federal courts have clear jurisdiction) or instead merely a state law cause of action (over which they do not have jurisdiction). This question frequently is a very important question. The choice from among our models provides the answer to this question. If the Legalist model's answer is adopted—"no constitutional cause of action when the 'laws' are constitutionally proper"—then, depending on the definition of "laws" that is chosen, a sizable number of cases may be precluded from reaching the dockets of the federal courts.

Second—and much more important, we believe, than considerations of federal case loads to which the choice of model is relevant—conceptual and analytical clarity with respect to the choice of model (and the implications and nonimplications of the choice) can easily avert doctrinal confusion, and unfortunate decisions spawned by confusion, in several areas in which confusion currently is present.

The first area is the constitutional merits of claims arising under permissive laws—the "state action" cases. No one disputes that "state action" doctrine is hopelessly muddled. And we believe that several cases—*Flagg Brothers, Inc., v. Brooks* (1978)[1] is a notable example—have been incorrectly decided because of that muddle. Our analysis of the models should eliminate the muddle, if not the other difficulties relating to value choices that attend such cases.

The second area is the choice of remedy and defendant for unconstitutional acts. The Supreme Court has often written as though finding someone to be a violator of the Constitution automatically made that person an appropriate target for constitutional remedies; and, as a corollary, as though finding someone not to be a violator of the Constitution automatically excluded that person from consideration as a target for constitutional remedies. Our analysis of the models and their implications exposes the Court's reasoning as mistaken, and thus may avert some erroneous decisions taken on its basis.[2]

The third area is the choice between federal forum and cause of action and state forum and cause of action. Our analysis has obvious implications for the multitude of cases involving violations of state law that are brought in federal court as constitutional violations. *Screws v. United States* (1945)[3] and *Monroe v. Pape* (1961),[4] and their progeny, are the most prominent examples. But several abstention cases also fall into this category.[5] The danger here is that confusion regarding the issue of the proper forum will spill over into the analysis of the substantive merits. The reader, in studying the cases in Appendix A that involve at bottom the forum issue, can make up her own mind whether this danger has been realized. We surely believe that it has.

As Appendix B illustrates, there is a fourth doctrinal area labeled as "constitutional torts" that involves the relation among (a) ordinary tort concepts like negligence, recklessness, and so forth, (b) the acts of government officials, and (c) constitutional principles. That area is currently quite confused.[6] Our analysis of the models can clarify the issues in that area, perhaps again averting erroneous decisions.

We believe that, by exposing the choice-of-models issue and analyzing its implications (primarily for federal-court versus state-court primary jurisdiction over claims relating to constitutional values)—and, perhaps much more importantly, its *non*implications (for the state-action/merits and remedies/defendants issues)—the Supreme Court and lower courts will be able to choose one model for each constitutional provision, define that model coherently, and apply that model consistently. In so doing those courts will, we predict, reach much sounder results than they have in the past on the constitutional merits of cases and on the constitutional adequacy of remedies for constitutional violations.

11

Postscript: Do Different Models Apply to Different Constitutional Provisions?

Despite suggestions planted here and there, the impression of our project thus far may be that: (1) the Constitution commands a narrow audience, a wide audience, or perhaps an audience of intermediate size; (2) having unveiled the models for the Constitution's referent, it is now up to someone—probably the Supreme Court—to select the *one* model from among them; (3) the selection, to have integrity, must be up-or-down for the Constitution as a whole; and (4) having made the selection of the one governing model for the Constitution's referent, everyone can set about articulating that model, solving the problems the model poses for particular cases or classes of cases, and so forth.

The Constitution, however, is a rather large document that serves many purposes and that speaks across a very broad range. That, at least, is the way it has come to be interpreted, not to mention amended. Is it not more plausible, then, to assume that different models for its referent apply to different constitutional provisions? A pluralistic view of the relationship of our models to the Constitution undoubtedly would prove more compatible than any monolithic view, both with the text of particular constitutional provisions and with the entirely appropriate attempt to preserve most (but never all) of the universe of its extant case law.

For example, some constitutional provisions by their terms impose duties on particular officials, such as the president.[1] Those provisions exclude all Naturalist models for their referent—at least in the form of making exceptions to a Naturalist model for the Constitution generally—and also strongly suggest a Governmental model as opposed to a Legalist or Legalist/Governmental hybrid model. On the other hand, the Legalist or Legalist hybrid models might seem the most appropriate to adopt for the

First, Fourteenth, and Fifteenth Amendments, given their structure and terms. And many have implicitly assumed—with at least some support in text—that the Naturalist model applies to the Thirteenth Amendment[2] and perhaps to dormant commerce clause cases,[3] although the Thirteenth Amendment on its face seems to express neutrality among the models, as does the commerce clause once the assumption is made that it imposes duties rather than serving merely as a source of congressional power.

The best that can be done with attempts to achieve universality, we believe, is to decide upon the model for whom the Constitution commands that is to be the presumptively correct one, leaving plenty of room in which to rebut the presumption on a provision-by-provision basis. We refuse to suggest the choice for presumption status, although our prior critiques must suggest a predilection for only the pure Legalist or Naturalist model. We have also suggested our belief that the least that should be accomplished, as a prelude to consistent and cogent constitutional interpretation, would be to settle upon one or another of the basic models as the governing model on a provision-by-provision basis.

In any event, we briefly describe how a provision-by-provision approach to our models for the Constitution's referent might enhance analysis.

THE THIRTEENTH AMENDMENT

The Supreme Court has suggested that the Thirteenth Amendment should be construed on the Naturalist model, that is, as speaking directly to and imposing duties directly upon private citizens.[4] And, indeed, Naturalists may derive support for such a view from the Thirteenth Amendment's text.[5]

Nevertheless, the rather extreme implications of the Naturalist model should lend credence to an alternative, Legalist-model view. On the Naturalist model, if A holds B against B's will, A has violated the Thirteenth Amendment even if A's act violates the laws of the state. The Naturalist easily would consider garden variety kidnapping and false imprisonment to be direct violations of the Thirteenth Amendment. (The same position could be taken, with very little effort beyond clearing away a handful of already suspect precedents, with respect to attempts to compel performance of personal service contracts.)[6] After all, the Thirteenth Amendment bans "involuntary servitude" in so many words. To the thoroughgoing Naturalist, the fact of involuntary servitude—not the fact that involuntary servitude was legally enforced by the slave states—is the essence of the "involuntary servitude" that was banned by the Thirteenth Amendment.

THE COMMERCE CLAUSE

On its face the commerce clause acts only as a grant of power to Congress.[7] Very early on, however, the Supreme court decided that state laws could violate the commerce clause by burdening interstate commerce.[8] Several theories were offered to explain how it was that state laws could violate the clause.

One theory has it that the clause itself bans state laws that are excessively burdensome to interstate commerce. The theory confronts the initial problem of lack of textual support. Another problem lies in how the theory could serve to justify the validation of congressional grants of power to the states to enact laws that previously had been found by the Supreme Court to burden commerce unconstitutionally.[9] After all, Congress has no power to authorize constitutional violations by the states.

A second theory attempts to square the view that the commerce clause speaks directly to the states with congressional grants of power to the states to enact laws burdening interstate commerce. The theory builds "congressional consent" into the text of the clause: the clause bars overly burdensome state regulation of interstate commerce to which Congress has not consented.

The second theory is only a short step away from yet a third theory, which views all invalidations of state law under the clause as premised on construction of congressional intent. This is the "silent will of Congress" theory.[10] On this theory, consent by Congress to a previously invalidated state law is mere correction of Supreme Court statutory misinterpretation (whereas, on the second theory, congressional consent is a necessary precondition for the constitutionality of the state law).

Regardless of which of these theories is thought to be most preferable, almost all of the commerce clause cases can be viewed on the Legalist model—that is, as concerned with state *law*. But in *In re Debs* (1895),[11] the Supreme Court laid the groundwork for a Naturalist-model extension of this commerce clause jurisprudence. In *Debs* the Court upheld a federal court's injunction against a railway strike, despite the absence of a federal statute authorizing such an injunction and the absence of any state law mandating the strike. In short, although Congress frequently legislates against private activity under the commerce clause, in *Debs* it had not done so; nor was there any state law that was burdening commerce. *Debs*, therefore, appears to be a Naturalist model case: Congress has exclusive power to regulate interstate commerce; the act of any person that unduly burdens interstate commerce—whether the "person" is a state, a government official, or a private citizen—is a constitutional violation (in the absence of congressional consent or ratification, and so forth).

THE FOURTH AMENDMENT

Although the language of the Fourth Amendment is neutral concerning choice of models,[12] it is possible to construe the amendment as adopting the pure Legalist model. On the Legalist model, the Fourth Amendment would speak only to the laws of the state that govern standards for both governmental and private searches and seizures, the training of police officers, and the rights of citizens to resist illegal arrests and searches. Then, if these state laws were constitutionally proper, a government official's (or private citizen's) violation of them would be an "illegal search and seizure" but not an "unconstitutional search and seizure."

Is it plausible to construe the Fourth Amendment on the Governmental model—that is, as speaking directly to government officials regardless of whether the laws are constitutional under which they are supposed to perform searches and seizures? On the Governmental model, the Fourth Amendment would be read as a direct command to any government official to refrain from searches and seizures without probable cause and warrants (when necessary), even if the law of the state includes the same commands and provides appropriate sanctions for violation of that law.

We believe that it is plausible to assume that some provisions of the Constitution—and the Fourth Amendment is a highly eligible candidate—speak directly to non-lawmaking persons who possess a certain legal authority. For example, the feature that distinguishes an illegal police search and seizure from an illegal private citizen search and seizure may be that the legal authority of the police is understood to preclude the victim's resistance to its illegal exercise. Moreover, possession by the police of such legal authority might well be consistent with the legal regime that is prescribed by the Fourth Amendment. Therefore, it is conceivable that the Fourth Amendment is concerned, not only with laws governing searches and seizures, but also with particular acts of searching and seizing when those acts are committed by persons possessing certain (constitutionally proper) legal authority.

Nevertheless, even in such a highly favorable environment as the Fourth Amendment, the Governmental model is threatened by collapse into either the Legalist or the Naturalist model. Thus, even the Fourth Amendment supports our view that the Governmental model, at best, is supported only by virtue of the compromise it may effect between the two extreme but principled models for the Constitution's referent. (Incidentally, the exchange we are about to unfold is applicable, not only to the Fourth Amendment, but as well to the commerce clause.)

On the Legalist side, the argument comes that possession of unusual legal authority is akin to having a limited lawmaking power. Thus, when the police engage in an illegal search and seizure, even one that seems to be illegal under state law, their act is one of lawmaking. Peculiar lawmaking, to be sure: it is contrary to higher order laws of the state; and it is valid only temporarily and only with respect to its restriction of the ordinary legal right of the victim to resist an illegal search and seizure. Nevertheless, whenever an act is one that can only be engaged in by one possessing unusual legal authority, the proponent of the Legalist model can deem it to be an act of lawmaking, and thus assimilate it into his model.[13]

On the Naturalist side, the rejoinder comes that *everyone,* without as well as within government, possesses special legal authority with respect to particular acts. A property owner has special legal authority with respect to her property. A parent has special legal authority with respect to her child. From these observations it can be made to follow that, if the Fourth Amendment is concerned with searches and seizures that are carried on by persons with special legal authority, then it is "persons with special legal authority"—not "government officials"—to whom the amendment speaks. And, if a private citizen has the legal authority to preclude ordinary resistance to her search and seizure, she too would be subject to the Fourth Amendment, regardless of whether she were part of government.

We already know that the Naturalist model encompasses the Legalist model.[14] The case of the Fourth Amendment illustrates how the Legalist model can be extended to encompass the Naturalist model. If the concept of "lawmaking" is expansive enough to encompass "abuse of legal authority," and if the concept of "legal authority" is expansive enough to encompass the legal powers possessed by private citizens, then any act that the Naturalist would deem to be unconstitutional can be labeled an act of lawmaking and deemed unconstitutional on the Legalist model.

It is clear, therefore, that although one may be led to prefer the Legalist model for the answer to the question of whom the Constitution commands—on grounds that the Governmental model is unstable and unprincipled, and that that Naturalist model has extreme (albeit principled) implications—the Legalist model will itself collapse into the others if it is not attended by adequate and principled criteria for "law" and "lawmaking." At the least, the Legalist model stands in constant danger of embracing all the problems of the Naturalist model within its principled universe.

THE MODELS CONTRASTED: A PRESCRIPTIVE EPILOGUE

The purpose of this book has been primarily to *describe* the choice of models by which to answer the question of whom the Constitution commands. We have refrained, wherever possible, from attempting to *prescribe* the choice. When all is said and done, however, we can make explicit two points of comparison that carry heavy prescriptive implications:

The Legalist model accords to the states—to their laws and to their courts—the greatest importance within the constitutional scheme, while the Naturalist model accords the least importance to the states.

The Legalist model is a fully principled model. The Naturalist model, likewise, is a fully principled model. Choice between them is a choice of governing principles.

The Governmental model is unprincipled; at best it represents an *ad hoc*—and ultimately unstable—compromise between the two more extreme yet principled models. And what is said of the Governmental model in this regard applies doubly and trebly to the three hybrid models that we also have described in this book.

Appendix A

A Look at Some Post-Civil War Supreme Court Decisions through the Prism of the Models of Whom the Constitution Commands

As we have explained in the preceding text, the Legalist model is the most restrictive of all models in its definition of whom the Constitution commands. For this reason, our main effort in this appendix is to indicate (1) the extent to which the Supreme Court cases we cite may be squared with the Legalist model (even though they may be squared, *a fortiori*, with other models for the Constitution's referent), and (2) the presence of language and analysis in the opinions that appears either to reject or to embrace models other than the Legalist Model.

In order to extrapolate appropriately from our discussion here, the following rules of thumb should be borne in mind: (1) All opinions holding there *is* "state action" are consistent, at least in their holdings, with the Naturalist model. (2) All opinions holding there is *no* "state action" are inconsistent with the Naturalist model, likely on grounds that some other model(s) have been implicitly employed in the opinion.

Informal citation to cases within Appendix A will be by bracketed references [] to numbered paragraphs.

FOURTEENTH AMENDMENT DECISIONS (CHRONOLOGICALLY)

1. United States v. Cruikshank, 92 U.S. 542 (1876). This was a criminal action prosecuted by the United States and brought against private defendants for conspiracy to interfere with blacks' constitutional rights, in violation of a federal statute. In the pertinent part of its decision, the Court held that the Fourteenth Amendment's due process and equal protection clauses placed duties only upon the states and not upon private individuals. The case appears explicitly to reject the Naturalist model.

2. Virginia v. Rives, 100 U.S. 313 (1879). The pertinent question in this case was whether black defendants could remove their state prosecution for murder to federal court because of racial discrimination in selecting their jury. Because the removal statute was available only for constitutional violations preceding trial, and the alleged violation here occurred after commencement of the trial, the Court denied removal.

The Court read the Virginia law as making illegal the act of the subordinate state official who discriminated in summoning potential jurors. Moreover, the Court expressed confidence that the Virginia judiciary would correct the problem on appeal (the trial court had convicted despite the claim of discrimination). Thus, on the Legalist model, there conceivably was no constitutional violation, though the matter is clouded because the officer's illegal act had the legal effect of forcing the defendants to go through a trial and part of a sentence before their convictions would be set aside by the higher state courts.

Because of the technicalities of the removal statute, the Court never had to face squarely the issue of whether the officer's illegal (on state law grounds) act was also a constitutional violation. In dictum, the Court waffled: "In one sense, indeed, his act was the act of the State, and was prohibited by the constitutional amendment. But inasmuch as it was a criminal misuse of state law, it cannot be said to have been such a 'denial or disability to enforce *in the judicial tribunals of the State*' the rights of colored men" (p. 321, emphasis in original). *See also* Bush v. Kentucky, 107 U.S. 110 (1882); *In re* Wood, 140 U.S. 278 (1891); Gibson v. Mississippi, 162 U.S. 565 (1896).

3. *Ex Parte* Virginia, 100 U.S. 339 (1879). This case is one of the strongest early precedents for a more comprehensive model than the Legalist model. It arose from a federal criminal prosecution of a Virginia county court judge for racial discrimination in jury selection. The Court upheld the constitutionality of applying the federal statue to the judge's alleged acts, stating that the Fourteenth Amendment applies to acts of states and, since states act only through agents, thereby to acts of the states' legislative, executive, and judicial officers. Because the Court had assumed in *Virginia v. Rives* [2] that Virginia law forbade racial discrimination in jury. Because the removal procedure was available only for constitutional model. Yet, because the Legalist model might count some improper judicial acts as "lawmaking," the adoption of the Governmental model is less than clear-cut. And the Court's language is itself no less ambiguous with respect to the choice of models (pp. 346-47):

> We have said the prohibitions of the Fourteenth Amendment are addressed to the States. They are, "No *State* shall make or enforce a law which shall abridge the privileges or immunities of citizens of the United States, . . . nor deny to any person within its jurisdiction the

equal protection of the laws.'' They have reference to actions of the political body denominated a State, by whatever instruments or in whatever modes that action may be taken. A State acts by its legislative, its executive, or its judicial authorities. It can act in no other way. The constitutional provision, therefore, must mean that no agency of the State, or of the officers or agents by whom its powers are exerted, shall deny to any person within its jurisdiction the equal protection of the laws. Whoever, by virtue of public position under a State government, deprives another of property, life, or liberty, without due process of law, or denies or takes away the equal protection of the laws, violates the constitutional inhibition; and as he acts in the name and for the State, and is clothed with the State's power, his act is that of the State. This must be so, or the constitutional prohibition has no meaning. Then the State has clothed one of its agents with power to annul or to evade it.

4. Neal v. Delaware, 103 U.S. 370 (1880). This case is similar factually to *Virginia v. Rives* [2], and involved the same federal removal statute. Likewise, the issue was racial discrimination in jury selection. The Delaware laws by their terms clearly limited service on juries to whites, but Delaware claimed that since the passage of the Civil War Amendments, the terms of its statutes had not been followed and that the true "law" of Delaware on juror selection was racially neutral. The Court assumed Delaware's color-blind interpretation of her law was correct. And although the Court denied that removal to federal court was proper, it held that racial discrimination by any state official in selecting jurors constituted a constitutional violation, and reversed the defendant's conviction.

The case can be read as consistent with the Legalist model in two different ways. First, Delaware's law on juror selection can be read to grant discretion to local officials, and the acts of the latter in selecting jurors could be deemed "lawmaking" acts. Alternatively, the Delaware court's acceptance of the jury panel despite the proof of discriminatory selection could be deemed the relevant act of lawmaking. Yet the case also quotes the paragraph in *Ex Parte Virginia* [3] that we quoted, suggesting adoption of the Governmental model. *See also* Norris v. Alabama, 294 U.S. 587 (1935).

5. United States v. Harris, 106 U.S. 629 (1883). The question here was whether a federal criminal statute predicated on Congress' power to enforce the Fourteenth Amendment could constitutionally be applied to private persons who beat up prisoners held for violations of state law. The Court followed *Cruikshank* [1] and explicitly rejected the Naturalist model. Because the state laws were proper, the Fourteenth Amendment was satisfied despite the beatings. The federal statute was therefore held to be unconstitutional.

6. Civil Rights Cases, 109 U.S. 3 (1883). Perhaps the most important early Court decision for our purposes, the *Civil Rights Cases* were a collection of challenges to the constitutionality of federal civil rights statutes insofar as they applied to private persons practicing racial discrimination in public accommodations. In holding the statutes unconstitutional, the Court explicitly rejected the Naturalist model as the proper model for the Fourteenth Amendment. (In dictum the Court also stated that the Naturalist model was inappropriate for Contract Clause cases [p. 10].)

Although the Court did not have to decide between the Legalist and Governmental models, most of the language points toward the former. Indeed, the Court read *Ex Parte Virginia* [3] as a case in which the officer who racially discriminated was expressing a rule of the state rather than violating such a rule (pp. 15-16).

The Court also did not decide whether state laws are unconstitutional that allow racial discrimination in privately owned public accommodations. Many commentators and courts, however, read the *Civil Rights Cases* as holding that such permissive laws are not unconstitutional because "no state action" is involved. That reading is not only incoherent; it is not the holding of the Court, and is indeed impliedly discountenanced in the following paragraph (pp. 17-18):

> In this connection it is proper to state that civil rights, such as are guaranteed by the Constitution against State aggression, cannot be impaired by the wrongful acts of individuals, unsupported by State authority in the shape of laws, customs, or judicial or executive proceedings. The wrongful act of an individual, unsupported by any such authority, is simply a private wrong, or a crime of that individual; an invasion of the rights of the injured party, it is true, whether they affect his person, his property, or his reputation; but if not sanctioned in some way by the State, or not done under State authority, his rights remain in full force, and may presumably be vindicated by resort to the laws of the State for redress. An individual cannot deprive a man of his right to vote, to hold property, to buy and sell, to sue in the courts, or to be a witness or a juror; he may, by force or fraud, interfere with the enjoyment of the right in a particular case; he may commit an assault against the person, or commit murder, or use ruffian violence at the polls, or slander the good name of a fellow citizen; but, unless protected in these wrongful acts by some shield of State law or State authority, he cannot destroy or injure the right; he will only render himself amenable to satisfaction or punishment; and amenable therefore to the laws of the State where the wrongful acts are committed. Hence, in all those cases where the Constitution seeks to protect the rights of the citizen against discriminative and unjust

laws of the State by prohibiting such laws, it is not individual offences, but abrogation and denial of rights, which it denounces, and for which it clothes the Congress with power to provide a remedy. This abrogation and denial of rights, for which the States alone were or could be responsible, was the great seminal and fundamental wrong which was intended to be remedied. And the remedy to be provided must necessarily be predicated upon that wrong. It must assume that in the cases provided for, the evil or wrong actually committed rests upon some State law or State authority for its excuse and perpetration.

The Court here surely appears to be saying that the constitutional defect in the federal statute consisted in employment of the wrong model of whom the Fourteenth Amendment commands—that is, in making the adequacy of the state laws totally irrelevant to finding a statutory violation—and did not consist in adopting the view that state permission of private discrimination in public accommodations is a constitutional violation.

7. Yick Wo v. Hopkins, 118 U.S. 356 (1886). This case can be viewed as operating exclusively within the Legalist model, standing for the proposition that where a statute or ordinance grants an official discretion, the exercise of that discretion results in a "law" for purposes of the Legalist model. *See also* The Japanese Immigrant Case, 189 U.S. 86 (1903). (Of course, like all cases in which a court deems an act unconstitutional despite the act's permissibility under state law, *Yick Wo* is consistent with the Governmental and Naturalist models.)

8. Scott v. McNeal, 154 U.S. 34 (1894). This case stands for the proposition that judicial action that is unappealable (final) under the law of the state is a "state action" subject to the Fourteenth Amendment. The case fits comfortably within the Legalist model and serves to define that model's boundary. The case was followed in Chicago, Burlington and Quincy Railroad Company v. Chicago, 166 U.S. 226 (1897).

9. Barney v. City of New York, 193 U.S. 430 (1904). This unanimous decision rejects the Governmental, and by implication the Naturalist, model for the Fourteenth Amendment. Plaintiff sued to enjoin defendant's construction of a subway adjacent to plaintiff's premises. Jurisdiction in the federal courts was asserted on the ground that the subway construction deprived plaintiff of property in violation of the due process clause. The Court denied federal court jurisdiction on the ground that defendant's action was illegal under state law and hence could not be deemed "state action" for Fourteenth Amendment purposes. *See also* Memphis v. Cumberland Telephone Co., 218 U.S. 624 (1910); Siler v. Louisville &

Nashville R.R. Co., 213 U.S. 175 (1909). For earlier cases foreshadowing the specific holding in *Barney*, see Arrowsmith v. Harmoning, 118 U.S. 194, 195 (1885); Hamilton Gas, Light and Coke Co. v. Hamilton City, 146 U.S. 258, 265-66 (1892).

10. Raymond v. Chicago Union Traction Company, 207 U.S. 20 (1907). This decision appears to us, as it did to Justice Holmes in dissent, to overrule *Barney* [9]. The Illinois board of equalization was alleged to have assessed the traction company's property in a discriminatory manner, in violation of both Illinois law and the Fourteenth Amendment. The Court held that there was federal jurisdiction despite the allegation that state law was violated, since the board was an arm of the state of Illinois and was acting in pursuance of its general authority under state law to assess property.

Justice Holmes dissented (p. 41):

> It seems to me that the appellee should not be heard until it has exhausted its local remedies; that the action of the state board of equalization should not be held to be the action of the State until, at least, it has been sanctioned directly, in a proceeding which the appellee is entitled to bring, by the final tribunal of the State, the Supreme Court. I am unable to grasp the principle on which the State is said to deprive the appellee of its property without due process of law because a subordinate board, subject to the control of the Supreme Court of the State, is said to have violated the express requirement of the State in its constitution; because, in other words, the board has disobeyed the authentic command of the State by failing to make its valuations in such a way that every person shall pay a tax in proportion to the value of his property. I should have thought that the action of the State was to be found in its constitution, and that no fault could be found with that until the authorized interpreter of that constitution, the Supreme Court, had said that it sanctioned the alleged wrong. *Barney v. New York,* 193 U.S. 430.

This case is another building block for the Governmental model of the Fourteenth Amendment, though the case might be consistent with some renditions of the Legalist model if the (state law) illegal assessments of the board had some legal authority under state law over and above ordinary illegal acts.

11. Home Telephone & Telegraph Company v. City of Los Angeles, 227 U.S. 278 (1913). This unanimous decision is the strongest support—to its date—for the Governmental model, at least where the act illegal under state law would be an act of lawmaking by lawmaking officials if it were not illegal under state law.

In the case, a Los Angeles ordinance was alleged to be confiscatory, in violation of both the Fourteenth Amendment and the California Constitution. The Court all but overruled *Barney* [9], followed *Raymond* [10], and held that the federal courts had jurisdiction to rule on the Fourteenth Amendment claim without awaiting state court consideration of the allegation of state law illegality.

The Court analogized the argument that the unconstitutionality of the ordinance under the state constitution rendered the ordinance not "state action" to the argument that federal unconstitutionality deprives any act of the status of "state action" (since no act in violation of the federal Constitution can be deemed lawful). The latter argument would strip the federal courts of jurisdiction over Fourteenth Amendment claims, an absurd result. And since the latter argument could not be correct, the Court argued that, by analogy, neither could the former.

12. Guinn v. United States, 238 U.S. 347 (1915), Myers v. Anderson, 238 U.S. 368 (1915), and Lane v. Wilson, 307 U.S. 268 (1939). (These cases arose under the Fifteenth Amendment, but the Court has consistently treated Fifteenth and Fourteenth Amendment cases as identical insofar as the choice of models is concerned.) All three cases involved suits against state officials for administering unconstitutional state statutes. *Guinn* involved a federal criminal prosecution; *Meyers* and *Lane* were civil suits for damages under a federal statute. The Court found no impediment to any of the suits.

The cases are consistent with the Legalist model, since under that model a federal remedy for lawmakers' violations of the Constitution (the constitutionally based remedial meta-regime) might lie against non-lawmaking officials. The cases are, of course, also consistent with the Governmental, the Legalist/Governmental, and Governmental/Naturalist models. Indeed the cases are consistent with all the models. *See also* Nixon v. Herndon, 273 U.S. 536 (1927) (Fourteenth Amendment).

13. Saunders v. Shaw, 244 U.S. 317 (1917). This unexceptional case was a precursor to *Shelley v. Kraemer* [24], in that Justice Holmes wrote for a unanimous Court that action taken by the state's supreme court could violate the Fourteenth Amendment exactly as if state legislation had dictated the result. Clearly the case fits within any plausible rendition of the Legalist model. *See also* Moore v. Dempsey, 261 U.S. 86 (1923).

14. Greene v. Louisville & Interurban Railroad Company, 244 U.S. 499 (1917). This was a suit for injunctive relief brought in federal court, with federal jurisdiction based on the presence of constitutional issues. The railroad contended that the defendants' assessment of their property, though within the state's statutory and constitutional guidelines, was above

the assessment rate employed by other state and local assessors in dealing with other taxpayers. The Court found that the action of the defendant assessors, though it violated state law by being inconsistent with other assessments, was state action for purposes of stating a cause of action based on the Fourteenth Amendment. (The Court ultimately disposed of the case on state law grounds and did not reach the Fourteenth Amendment issue.)

The case could be read as endorsing the Governmental model. Yet, because the state supreme court had held on similar facts that while the variation in tax rates amounted to a violation of state law, no redress was available in the state courts (pp. 512-13), the case can also be read as consistent with the Legalist model, with the remedial laws of the state being (federally) constitutionally defective. Interestingly, the Court based its holding for the taxpayers on the substantive state law, ignoring its state court remedial limitations (p. 513).

15. Corrigan v. Buckley, 271 U.S. 323 (1926). This case presented facts similar to those in *Shelley v. Kraemer* [24]; but in *Corrigan* the Court, per Justice Sanford (and without dissent), held that no substantial federal question was presented by the defendants' contention that enforcement of a racially restrictive covenant would violate the Fourteenth Amendment. The Court held that the covenant itself was not state action, impliedly rejecting the Naturalist model as proper in Fourteenth Amendment cases. But the Court also held (incorrectly) that judicial enforcement of the covenant was not state action, a position later rejected by *Shelley*.

16. Brinkerhoff-Faris Trust & Savings Company v. Hill, 281 U.S. 673 (1930). In this case the plaintiff brought an injunctive action in state court against a county tax collector, alleging the assessment of its property was discriminatory, in violation both of state law and the Fourteenth Amendment. The Supreme Court held that action by the Missouri courts denying relief—by overruling a precedent holding that exhaustion of administrative remedies was not required in the circumstances, then holding that plaintiff was guilty of laches in not pursuing administrative relief—was state action. The case is consistent with the Legalist model, given the assumption that Missouri courts are "lawmakers."

17. Iowa–Des Moines National Bank v. Bennett, 284 U.S. 239 (1931). Another discriminatory taxation case, again presenting a violation of state law. Here the Court unanimously held that the actions of the taxing officials were "state action" for Fourteenth Amendment purposes, despite their illegality under state law. The Court expressly relied on *Home Telephone & Telegraph* [11] and seemed at that point to come down foursquare for the Governmental model. Nonetheless, the Court's endorsement of the Governmental model is clouded by the final paragraph

of its opinion, which can be read as holding the state's remedial laws to be constitutionally defective, which holding in turn would square the case with the Legalist model (p. 247, emphasis ours):

> The fact that the State may still have power to equalize the treatment of the petitioners and the competing domestic corporations by compelling the latter to pay hereafter the unpaid balance of the amounts assessed against them in 1919, 1920, 1921, and 1922 is not material. The petitioners' rights were violated, and the causes of action arose, when taxes at the lower rate were collected from their competitors. *It may be assumed that all ground for a claim for refund would have fallen if the State, promptly upon discovery of the discrimination, had removed it by collecting the additional taxes from the favored competitors. By such collection the petitioners' grievances would have been redressed;* for these are not primarily overassessment. The right invoked is that to equal treatment; and such treatment will be attained if either their competitors' taxes are increased or their own reduced. But it is well settled that a taxpayer who has been subjected to discriminatory taxation through the favoring of others in violation of federal law, cannot be required himself to assume the burden of seeking an increase of the taxes which the others should have paid. . . . Nor may he be remitted to the necessity of awaiting such action by the state officials upon their own initiative.

18. Nixon v. Condon, 286 U.S. 73 (1932). This case stands for the proposition that when state law designates a body to determine political party membership (and hence the ability to vote in the party's primary) independently of the will of the party members, the acts of that body are "state action" subject to the Fourteenth Amendment. The case is consistent with any plausible rendition of the Legalist model.

19. Mooney v. Holohan, 294 U.S. 103 (1935). This interesting case involved a convicted defendant's allegations that the state prosecutor had secured his conviction through use of perjured testimony and suppression of exculpatory evidence. Unquestionably such action was illegal under state law. But the question of whether either the prosecutor's acts, or the state court's conviction in such circumstances, violated the Fourteenth Amendment was never squarely faced because the Court held that state relief through unexhausted state remedial procedures was still available. Thus, no clear choice of models emerges from the decision. *But see* Chessman v. Teets, 350 U.S. 3 (1955) (petition for a federal writ of habeas corpus on similar allegations states a basis for federal relief from a constitutional violation; remedial options not discussed by Court, implying the official's act was "state action" despite being illegal); Imbler v. Pachtman, 424 U.S. 409 (1976) (prosecutors absolutely immune from

federal liability for knowingly suppressing evidence or using tainted evidence, implying that such acts constitute constitutional violations regardless of their status under state law).

20. Hague v. Committee for Industrial Organization, 310 U.S. 496 (1939). In this case, the Court upheld an injunction forbidding city officials from acting under an unconstitutional ordinance. The case is consistent with the Legalist model, either because the actions of officials in enforcing laws is lawmaking, or because the constitutional remedial meta-regime authorizes injunctive relief against those officials in certain circumstances when the lawmakers have enacted unconstitutional laws. Of course, the case is also consistent with all the other models.

21. Smith v. Allwright, 321 U.S. 649 (1944). In this case, a black sued Texas officials for damages under federal law for denying him his constitutional rights by refusing to permit him to vote in the Democratic primary. Texas law permitted the Democratic party to determine who was eligible to vote in its primary, and the party had excluded blacks. The Court held that Texas' extensive regulation of primary elections and political parties made the act of the Democratic party excluding blacks "state action." As such it violated the Fifteenth Amendment, and the suit was allowed to go forth.

The case can be squared with the Legalist model in two ways. First, the authority granted to the Democratic party and the regulation of the party by the state may have justified the Court's holding that the party's act of excluding blacks from membership was tantamount to a lawmaking act under an expansive rendition of the Legalist model. Alternatively, the laws of Texas regulating and granting authority to the party, rather than the acts of the party itself, may have been the constitutionally defective lawmaking acts for purposes of the Legalist model. In the latter case, the officials sued would not be liable as constitutional violators, but perhaps liable under a proper remedial meta-regime (remedies for constitutional violations by lawmakers). Of course, Smith is also consistent with the other models. See also Gray v. Sanders, 372 U.S. 368 (1963).

22. Screws v. United States, 325 U.S. 91 (1945). This case is one of the major precedents for the Governmental model. A sheriff, a deputy sheriff, and a policeman were indicted under federal law for violating a prisoner's constitutional rights by beating him to death, apparently because of a personal grudge, while he was in their custody. Their act was clearly a violation of state law, and there was no evidence adduced that the state would not apply its law to the defendants, or that its law was in any other sense constitutionally defective. Nonetheless, Justice Douglas, writing for the majority, found state action (p. 111):

We are not dealing here with a case where an officer not authorized to act nevertheless takes action. Here the state officers were authorized to make an arrest and to take such steps as were necessary to make the arrest effective. They acted without authority only in the sense that they used excessive force in making the arrest effective. It is clear that under "color" of law means under "pretense" of law. Thus acts of officers in the ambit of their personal pursuits are plainly excluded. Acts of officers who undertake to perform their official duties are included whether they hew to the line of their authority or overstep it. If, as suggested, the statute was designed to embrace only action which the State in fact authorized, the words "under color of any law" were hardly apt words to express the idea.

Justice Rutledge, concurring, elaborated on defendants' "no state action" argument (pp. 114-117, footnotes omitted):

[T]heir argument now admits the offense, but insists it was against the state alone, not the nation. So they have made their case in this Court.

In effect, the position urges it is murder they have done, not deprivation of constitutional right. Strange as the argument is the reason. It comes to this, that abuse of state power creates immunity to federal power. Because what they did violated the state's laws, the nation cannot reach their conduct. It may deprive the citizen of his liberty and his life. But whatever state officers may do in abuse of their official capacity can give this Government and its courts no concern. This, though the prime object of the Fourteenth Amendment and Sect. 20 [the federal statute] was to secure these fundamental rights against wrongful denial by exercise of the power of the states.

The defense is not pretty. Nor is it valid. By a long course of decision from *Ex parte Virginia*, 100 U.S. 339, to *United States v. Classic*, 313 U.S. 299, it has been rejected. The ground should not need ploughing again. It was cleared long ago and thoroughly. It has been kept clear, until the ancient doubt, laid in the beginning, was resurrected in the last stage of this case. The evidence has nullified any pretense that petitioners acted as individuals, about their personal though nefarious business. They used the power of official place in all that was done. The verdict has foreclosed semblance of any claim that only private matters, not touching official functions, were involved. Yet neither was the state's power, they say.

There is no third category. The Amendment and the legislation were not aimed at rightful state action. Abuse of state power was the target. Limits were put to state authority, and states were forbidden to pass them, by whatever agency. It is too late now, if there were better reason than exists for doing so, to question that in these matters abuse

binds the state and is its act, when done by one to whom it has given
power to make the abuse effective to achieve the forbidden ends.
Vague ideas of dual federalism, of ultra vires doctrine imported from
private agency, and of want of finality in official action, do not nullify
what four years of civil strife secured and eighty years have verified.
For it was abuse of basic civil and political rights, by states and their
officials, that the Amendment and the enforcing legislation were
adopted to uproot.

The danger was not merely legislative or judicial. Nor was it
threatened only from the state's highest officials. It was abuse by
whatever agency the state might invest with its power capable of
inflicting the deprivation. In all its flux, time makes some things
axiomatic. One has been that state officials who violate their oaths of
office and flout the fundamental law are answerable to it when their
misconduct brings upon them the penalty it authorizes and Congress
has provided.

There could be no clearer violation of the Amendment or the
statute. No act could be more final or complete, to denude the victim
of rights secured by the Amendment's very terms. Those rights so
destroyed cannot be restored. Nor could the part played by the state's
power in causing their destruction be lessened, though other organs
were now to repudiate what was done. The state's law might thus be
vindicated. If so, the vindication could only sustain, it could not
detract from the federal power. Nor could it restore what the federal
power shielded. Neither acquittal nor conviction, though affirmed by
the state's highest court, could resurrect what the wrongful use of
state power has annihilated. There was in this case abuse of state
power, which for the Amendment's great purposes was state action,
final in the last degree, depriving the victim of his liberty and his life
without due process of law.

(In the footnotes, Rutledge cites to the various cases mentioned above that
lend support to the Governmental model.)

As we have discussed, illegal acts by police officers while otherwise
performing their duties may be capable of being deemed lawmaking acts
within an expansive version of the Legalist model. Their illegal acts may
carry some force of law that illegal acts by others would not carry. But
surely the line between such a version of the Legalist model and the
Governmental model is blurred, if it exists at all.

Justice Roberts, joined by Frankfurter and Jackson, dissented on this
point (pp. 147-48):

It has never been satisfactorily explained how a State can be said to
deprive a person of liberty or property without due process of law
when the foundation of the claim is that a minor official has

disobeyed the authentic command of his State. See *Raymond v. Chicago Traction Co.,* 207 U.S. 20, 40, 41. Although action taken under such circumstances has been deemed to be deprivation by a "State" of rights guaranteed by the Fourteenth Amendment for purposes of federal jurisdiction, the doctrine has had a fluctuating and dubious history. Compare *Barney v. City of New York,* 193 U.S. 430, with *Raymond v. Chicago Traction Co., supra; Memphis v. Cumberland Telephone Co.,* 218 U.S. 624, with *Home Tel. & Tel. Co. v. Los Angeles,* 227 U.S. 278. *Barney v. City of New York, supra,* which ruled otherwise, although questioned, has never been overruled. See, for instance, *Iowa-Des Moines Bank v. Bennett,* 284 U.S. 239, 246-247, and *Snowden v. Hughes,* 321 U.S. 1, 13.

See also Williams v. United States, 341 U.S. 97 (1951).

23. Marsh v. Alabama, 326 U.S. 501 (1946). This famous case, although perhaps controversial on its merits, poses no problems for the Legalist model. On that model, the trespass law of Alabama, as applied to protect the property rights of a company town against peaceful leafletting, violated the Fourteenth Amendment. Mrs. Marsh's conviction under that law, affirmed by the state's highest court, was reversed by the Supreme Court.

24. Shelley v. Kraemer, 334 U.S. 1 (1948). This case, even more than *Marsh* [23], is controversial on its merits, but like *Marsh*, it is unproblematic insofar as the Legalist model is concerned. The question was whether the Missouri law of covenants was constitutional as applied to racially restrictive covenants. The Court held it was not. There was no question that the acts of the Missouri courts insofar as they established what the law of Missouri was were lawmaking acts. *See also* Barrows v. Jackson, 346 U.S. 249 (1953); New York Times v. Sullivan, 376 U.S. 254 (1964) (and progeny); Zacchini v. Scripps-Howard Broadcasting Co., 433 U.S. 562 (1977); Martinez v. California, 444 U.S. 277 (1980); NAACP v. Claiborne Hardware Co., 458 U.S. 886 (1982).

25. Terry v. Adams, 345 U.S. 461 (1953). This was a suit by black citizens of a Texas county against an organized, whites-only voting bloc of the Democratic party in the county. The claim was that the organization's exclusion of blacks violated the Fifteenth Amendment. The Court held for the black citizens, though the majority opinion is ambiguous regarding whether the state's laws violated the Constitution (by permitting the racial policy), or alternatively whether the organization's whites-only policy violated the Constitution. The latter holding would imply the Naturalist, Legalist/Naturalist, or Governmental/Naturalist model. (On the merits the decision is quite problematic, at least insofar as it implies that racially and

perhaps religiously and sexually exclusive political parties are constitutionally forbidden. *See* Justice Minton's dissent, pp. 493-94.)

26. Pennsylvania v. Board of Directors of City Trusts, 353 U.S. 230
(1957). In this Per Curiam decision, the Court held that the City of
Philadelphia's administration of a racially discriminatory private trust
violated the Fourteenth Amendment. The case is comfortably within the
Legalist model—assuming trust administration, and its attendant demands
on official personnel and resources, constitutes lawmaking—though more
interesting and difficult on its merits than the short opinion would suggest.

27. United States v. Raines, 362 U.S. 17 (1960). This is another case that
supports the Governmental model. It involved a federal prosecution of state
voting officials for racial discrimination. The defendants contended that
theirs was not "state action" because it might be corrected by higher state
officials or the state courts, citing *Barney* [9]. The Court deemed *Barney* a
dead letter; but in a footnote (p. 26 n. 6), it also distinguished *Barney* on the
ground that in *Barney* it was clear that the state had outlawed the activity
and was prepared to provide a remedy, implying that in *Raines,* the
defendants' acts were not on their face illegal or remediable *on state law
grounds*.

28. Monroe v. Pape, 365 U.S. 167 (1961). This is the most important
Supreme Court decision in support of the Governmental model. The
question of interest in the case was whether police officers acted "under
color of law" and violated the Fourteenth Amendment by conducting an
outrageous arrest and search that were illegal and remediable under state
law. Justice Douglas, writing for the majority, relied on *Screws* [22], and
held that the police officers violated Fourteenth Amendment rights.

Justice Harlan, joined by Justice Stewart, expressed some doubt about
the holding in *Screws*, but concurred on the basis on *stare decisis*. Harlan
did argue, in support of *Screws*, that he could see no difference between
state court remedies for state law violations and state court remedies for
constitutional violations. If the former were adequate to negate the
constitutional violation, why not the latter? The response to Harlan is, of
course, that a state court remedy for a constitutional violation assumes that
there *is* a constitutional violation; the remedy can hardly negate the
existence of that for which it is a remedy. Harlan's confusion here is not
original; Chief Justice White was guilty of the same mistake in *Home
Telephone & Telegraph* [11]. *See* 277 U.S. at p. 285.

Justice Frankfurter wrote a powerful dissent, arguing at great length the
position he had supported in *Screws*. The analytical (as opposed to
historical) heart of his dissent is captured in the following passages (pp.
242-55):

In concluding that police intrusion in violation of state law is not a wrong remediable under R. S. Sect. 1979, the pressures which urge an opposite result are duly felt. The difficulties which confront private citizens who seek to vindicate in traditional common-law actions their state-created rights against lawless invasion of their privacy by local policemen are obvious, and obvious is the need for more effective modes of redress. The answer to these urgings must be regard for our federal system which presupposes a wide range of regional autonomy in the kinds of protection local residents receive. If various common-law concepts make it possible for a policeman—but no more possible for a policeman than for any individual hoodlum intruder—to escape without liability when he has vandalized a home, that is an evil. But, surely, its remedy devolves, in the first instance, on the States. Of course, if the States afford less protection against the police, as police, than against the hoodlum—if under authority of state "statute, ordinance, regulation, custom, or usage" the police are specially shielded—Sect. 1979 provides a remedy which dismissal of petitioners' complaint in the present case does not impair. Otherwise, the protection of the people from local delinquencies and shortcomings depends, as in general it must, upon the active consciences of state executives, legislators and judges. Federal intervention, which must at best be limited to securing those minimal guarantees afforded by the evolving concepts of due process and equal protection, may in the long run do the individual a disservice by deflecting responsibility from the state lawmakers, who hold the power of providing a far more comprehensive scope of protection. Local society, also, may well be the loser, by relaxing its sense of responsibility and, indeed, perhaps resenting what may appear to it to be outside interference where local authority is ample and more appropriate to supply needed remedies. . . .

This meaning, no doubt, poses difficulties for the case-by-case application of Sect. 1979. Manifestly the applicability of the section in an action for damages cannot be made to turn upon the actual availability or unavailability of a state-law remedy for each individual plaintiff's situation. Prosecution to adverse judgment of a state-court damage claim cannot be made prerequisite to Sect. 1979 relief. In the first place, such a requirement would effectively nullify Sect. 1979 as a vehicle for recovering damages. In the second place, the conclusion that police activity which violates state law is not "under color" of state law does not turn upon the existence of a state tort remedy. Rather, it recognizes the freedom of the States to fashion their own laws of torts in their own way under no threat of federal intervention save where state law makes determinative of a plaintiff's rights the particular circumstances that defendants are acting by state authority.

Section 1979 was not designed to cure and level all the possible imperfections of local common-law doctrines, but to provide for the case of the defendant who can claim that some particular dispensation of state authority immunizes him from the ordinary processes of the law.

It follows that federal courts in actions at law under Sect. 1979 would have to determine whether defendants' conduct is in violation of, or under color of, state law often with little guidance from earlier state decisions. Such a determination will sometimes be difficult, of course. But Federal District Courts sitting in diversity cases are often called upon to determine as intricate and uncertain questions of local law as whether official authority would cloak a given practice of the police from liability in a state-court suit. Certain fixed points of reference will be available. If a plaintiff can show that defendant is acting pursuant to the specific terms of a state statute or of a municipal ordinance, Sect. 1979 will apply. See *Lane v. Wilson*, 307 U.S. 268. If he can show that defendant's conduct is within the range of executive discretion in the enforcement of a state statute, or municipal ordinance, Sect. 1979 will apply. See *Hague v. C. I. O.*, 307 U.S. 496. Beyond these cases will lie the admittedly more difficult ones in which he seeks to show some "'custom or usage' which has become common law." . . .

In truth, to deprecate the purposes of this 1871 statute in terms of analysis which refers to "merely . . . jurisdictional" effects, to "shifting the load of federal supervision," and to the "administrative burden on the Supreme Court," is to attribute twentieth century conceptions of the federal judicial system to the Reconstruction Congress. If today Congress were to devise a comprehensive scheme for the most effective protection of federal constitutional rights, it might conceivably think in terms of defining those classes of cases in which Supreme Court review of state-court decision was most appropriate, and those in which original federal jurisdiction was most appropriate, fitting all cases into one or the other category. The Congress of 1871 certainly did not think in such terms. Until 1875 there was no original "federal question" jurisdiction in the federal courts, and the ordinary mode of protection of federal constitutional rights was Supreme Court review. In light of the then prevailing notions of the appropriate relative spheres of jurisdiction of state and federal courts of first impression, any allowance of Federal District and Circuit Court competence to adjudicate causes between co-citizens of a State was a very special case, a rarity. To ask why, when such a special case was created to redress deprivations of federal rights under authority of state laws which abridged those rights, a special case was not also created to cover other deprivations of federal rights whose somewhat similar nature might have made the same redress appropriate, disregards the dominant jurisdictional thought of the day and neglects consideration of the fact that redress in a federal trial court was then to be very sparingly afforded. To extend original federal jurisdiction only in the class of cases in which, constitutional violation being sanctioned by state law, state judges would be less likely than federal judges to be sympathetic to a plaintiff's claim, is a purpose quite consistent with the "overflowing protection of constitutional rights" which, assuredly, Sect. 1979 manifests.

Finally, it seems not unreasonable to reject the suggestion that state-sanctioned constitutional violations are no more offensive than violations not sanctioned by the majesty of state authority. Degrees of offensiveness, perhaps, lie largely in the eye of the person offended, but is it implausible to conclude that there is something more reprehensible, something more dangerous, in the action of the custodian of a public building who turns out a Negro pursuant to a local ordinance than in the action of the same custodian who turns out the same Negro, in violation of state law, to vent a personal bias? Or something more reprehensible about the public officer who beats a criminal suspect under orders from the Captain of Detectives, pursuant to a systematic and accepted custom of third-degree practice, than about the same officer who, losing his temper, breaks all local regulations and beats the same suspect? If it be admitted that there is a significant difference between the situation of the individual injured by another individual and who, although the latter is an agent of the State, can claim from the State's judicial or administrative processes the same protection and redress against him as would be available against any other individual, and the situation of one who, injured under the sanction of a state law which shields the offender, is left alone and helpless in the face of the asserted dignity of the State, then, certainly, it was the latter of these two situations—that of the unprotected Southern Negroes and Unionists—about which Congress was concerned in 1871.

See also Bivens v. Six Unknown Named Agents of Federal Bureau of Narcotics, 403 U.S. 388 (1971).

29. Burton v. Wilmington Parking Authority, 365 U.S. 715 (1961). Like most cases labeled "state action" cases, *Burton* is interesting on the merits but comfortably within the Legalist model. The suit, predicated on the Fourteenth Amendment, sought to enjoin a private restaurant, leasing space in a municipally owned building, from practicing racial discrimination. The state supreme court denied relief. The Supreme Court reversed. The case fits within the Legalist model on the assumption that the

state violated the Fourteenth Amendment in permitting its lessee to discriminate. *See also* Turner v. Memphis, 369 U.S. 350 (1962).

30. McNeese v. Board of Education, 373 U.S. 668 (1963). In this case the Court held that the mere allegation that *de jure* segregated schools were illegal under Illinois law did not require exhaustion of state administrative remedies before resort to federal court. The Court relied on *Monroe v. Pape* [28], but it also expressed doubt over the adequacy of Illinois' remedies. The case supports the Governmental model, though the inadequacy of state remedies would bring it within the Legalist model. *See also* Patsy v. Florida Board of Regents, 457 U.S. 496 (1982) (state law status of officials' acts not mentioned but probably illegal, therefore supporting Governmental model); Damico v. California, 389 U.S. 416 (1967).

31. Griffin v. Maryland, 378 U.S. 130 (1964). In this case the issue was whether a state official—a deputy sheriff—could arrest blacks for trespass in pursuance of a security contract with a private amusement park that specifically directed him to exclude blacks from the premises. The Court held that the official's act was unconstitutional state action, relying on *Pennsylvania v. Board of Directors of City Trusts* [26]. The Court distinguished between the case of a private landowner's calling the police to arrest black trespassers as trespassers—presumably permissible—and the landowner's contracting with the police specifically to evict and/or arrest black trespassers. The distinction was too ephemeral for Justices Harlan, Black, and White, who dissented.

The case, like *Shelley v. Kraemer* [24] and *Pennsylvania v. Board of Directors of City Trusts,* is interesting on its merits, but fits snugly within the Legalist model.

32. Evans v. Newton, 382 U.S. 296 (1966). This is another famous "state action" case that, while difficult on its merits, may be understood as squarely within the Legalist model. A tract of land had been devised to a city to be operated as a segregated public park. The city did use the land as a segregated park for several years. When legal developments made it clear that the city could not continue legally operating a segregated park, it resigned as trustee, and the state court appointed private trustees. The Supreme Court held that past and present city involvement with the park made it violative of the Fourteenth Amendment for even private trustees to operate the park on a segregated basis. *See also* Evans v. Abney, 396 U.S. 435 (1970) (upholding the termination of the charitable trust involved in *Evans v. Newton*).

33. United States v. Guest, 383 U.S. 745 (1966). This was a federal prosecution of private individuals for conspiring to violate the

constitutional rights of blacks. Although the Court declared, citing *The Civil Rights Cases* [6], that the Fourteenth Amendment does not create rights of private citizens against other private citizens, but creates rights only against the state (p. 755), the Court found that defendants' harassing blacks by filing false reports of their criminal activity constituted sufficient involvement with state machinery to get past the state action requirement. The Court also held that the federal right to travel could be infringed by private persons acting with the purpose of so infringing that right.

Guest is one of the few authoritative supports for the Naturalist model. The cases relied upon—*Shelley v. Kraemer* [24], *Pennsylvania v. Board of Directors of City Trusts* [26], *Burton v. Wilmington Parking Authority* [29], *Griffin v. Maryland* [31], and *Evans v. Newton* [32]—while problematic in their own right, all involved situations in which the state knowingly enforced the discriminatory policies of private citizens. In *Guest*, however, no improper policies of the state were utilized. Filing false reports of crime no more involves the state than does using a public road to escape from the scene of a crime, or drowning someone in a public swimming pool.

Moreover, the right-to-travel portion of the holding is incoherent. If the federal right to travel is a right not to have certain local, state, or federal laws or policies that interfere with travel, then private citizens cannot logically interfere with such a right no matter what they do or intend; only lawmakers can do so. On the other hand, if the federal right to travel is, as the court said in *Guest,* a right against private citizens' acts accompanied by the specific intent to interfere with the federal right to travel, the right is fatally self-referential.

See also United States v. Price, 383 U.S. 787 (1966).

34. Reitman v. Mulkey, 387 U.S. 369 (1967). This, like many of the decisions noted above, is very perplexing on its merits, but comfortably within the Legalist model. California, through an initiative measure, repealed its fair housing laws and constitutionalized the right of real-property owners to deal with whomever they desired. The Court held this constitutional provision to be a violation of the equal protection clause, though *not* because state fair housing laws are constitutionally required, *not* because once enacted, state fair housing laws cannot be repealed, and *not* because states may not constitutionalize the right of real-property owners to deal only with those with whom they choose. *See also* Hunter v. Erickson, 393 U.S. 385 (1969).

35. Amalgamated Food Employees Union v. Logan Valley Plaza, 391 U.S. 308 (1968). This case involved state enforcement of its trespass laws against union picketers picketing on the premises of a privately owned shopping center against the wishes of the property owner. A divided Court held this application of the trespass law to abridge free speech, a holding later

restricted in Lloyd Corporation v. Tanner, 407 U.S. 551 (1972), and reversed in Hudgens v. N.L.R.B., 424 U.S. 507 (1976). (*See also* Central Hardware v. N.L.R.B., 407 U.S. 539 [1972].) Because the case involved holding a state law unconstitutional as applied, it raises no problem for the Legalist model.

36. Adickes v. S. H. Kress & Company, 398 U.S. 144 (1970). This case involved a suit for damages under section 1983 against a private department store for racially motivated refusal to serve. Relying on *United States v. Price* [33], *Monroe v. Pape* [28], and *Screws v. United States* [22], the Court held that the allegation of a conspiracy between the defendant and a state official to have plaintiff arrested on bogus charges was a sufficient allegation of "state action" to sustain the suit under 1983. *See also* Dennis v. Sparks, 449 U.S. 24 (1980); Tower v. Glover, 467 U.S. 914 (1984). The Court also held that despite the lack of laws compelling racial discrimination on their face, a state-enforced custom of requiring racial discrimination could constitute unconstitutional state action.

The latter holding in the case fits within the Legalist model, at least if what the Court was referring to was unwritten state common law. The federal suit against the private defendant, rather than suggesting the Naturalist model, or any of its hybrids, would be consistent with the Legalist model as a remedial suit (remedial meta-regime) for a constitutional violation by lawmaking officials. The former holding, like the holdings in *Guest* and *Price* [33], is, however, impossible to reconcile with the Legalist model if the state laws, written or unwritten, need not be alleged to be constitutionally infirm. That is, as a suit alleging that the defendants acted unconstitutionally, rather than as a suit seeking a remedy for unconstitutional acts of lawmakers, the suit suggests the Naturalist or Governmental/Naturalist model.

37. Moose Lodge No. 107 v. Irvis, 407 U.S. 163 (1972). This is another well-known "state action" case that is problem-free for the Legalist model, whatever problems it has on the merits. At issue was the constitutionality of Pennsylvania's granting Moose Lodge No. 107 a liquor license while at the same time permitting it to discriminate racially. The Court found Pennsylvania's legal regime to be constitutionally permissible in these respects.

38. Norwood v. Harrison, 413 U.S. 455 (1973). This is still another "state action" case that, while interesting on its merits, poses no problem for the Legalist model. The Court held that Mississippi's lending of textbooks to private schools that barred blacks violated the equal protection clause and could be enjoined. *See also* Gilmore v. City of Montgomery, 417 U.S. 556 (1974).

39. Jackson v. Metropolitan Edison Company, 419 U.S. 345 (1974). In still another interesting and controversial "state action" case, the Court held that extensive state regulation and protection (from competition) of a privately owned public utility did not convert the utility's termination of service to a customer into an act subject to the due process clause. The case obviously is consistent with the Legalist model.

40. O'Connor v. Donaldson, 422 U.S. 563 (1975). In this case the Court held that the involuntary confinement without treatment in a state mental hospital of one alleged to be mentally ill but not dangerous to self or others violated the due process clause and subjected the superintendent of the hospital to federal damages liability. The superintendent apparently was exercising discretion granted by state law in refusing to release the inmate. Thus, under the Legalist model the superintendent could be considered a lawmaker, one who had the power to breach a constitutional duty. (Even if the superintendent were not a lawmaker, he might still be the appropriate target for remedial action under the Legalist model if the laws of the state that he administered were unconstitutional.)

41. Estelle v. Gamble, 429 U.S. 97 (1976). In this case a prisoner brought a section 1983 action against state prison officials for deliberate neglect of his medical needs. The Court held that such deliberate neglect was unconstitutional and that a federal suit against officials could be predicated on such neglect.

The Court did not discuss whether the action of the officials was proscribed by state law, but it did distinguish between medical malpractice by the prison physician, which it held to be actionable only under state law, and the deliberate indifference of other, nonmedical prison officials, which it held was unconstitutional state action. If the implication of the distinction is that the acts of the latter were acts of discretionary lawmaking, then the case comes within the Legalist model. If not, then the case is a confusing combination of (1) the Governmental model with respect to (state-law-proscribed) intentional and reckless disregard of prisoner needs, and (2) either (a) a Legalist model, or else (b) a finding of no invasion of a constitutionally protected interest, with respect to (state-law-proscribed) negligent disregard of those needs.

The latter possibility was apparently renounced in those recent cases that refused to distinguish negligent invasion of constitutional interests from intentional and reckless invasions—*see Parratt v. Taylor* [44] and *Hudson v. Palmer* [49]—but then reinstated with respect to cruel and unusual punishment in Whitley v. Albers, 106 S. Ct. 1078 (1986), and perhaps generally with respect to the due process clauses in *Daniels v. Williams* and *Davidson v. Cannon* [52].

42. Flagg Brothers, Inc., v. Brooks, 436 U.S. 149 (1978). This was a suit by a bailor against her bailee under section 1983 seeking to enjoin sale of the items in storage. The bailor's claim was that sale of the items under New York's Uniform Commercial Code Section 7-210 would be state action violative of the due process clause. Justice Rehnquist, writing for the majority of five, held that defendant Flagg Brothers was not a state actor and thus could not be sued for "acting under color of . . . law."

Justice Rehnquist was surely correct if one adopts the Legalist model. However, the fact that Flagg Brothers was not a bearer of Fourteenth Amendment duties did not necessarily require dismissal of the section 1983 suit. Rehnquist would have to have held, in addition, that section 1983 is not a proper vehicle for remedying the effects of unconstitutional state laws when the defendant is acting under those unconstitutional state laws. In fact, later, in *Lugar v. Edmundson Oil Co.* [48], the court distinguished between those who can violate the Constitution and those who can be sued under section 1983 for "acting under color of" unconstitutional state laws.

Justice Rehnquist had another arrow in his quiver. He implied that permissive state laws could never constitute unconstitutional state action. He attempted to distinguish other laws permitting creditors to seize debtors' property that had been struck down as violative of due process. His basis for distinction was that in every case in which the state debtor/creditor laws were struck down, the creditor had acted with the aid of some state official or state court (pp. 160-61 n. 10). But surely this is an indefensible basis for refusing to assess the merits of section 7-210, since there was absolutely no reason to suppose that the New York courts would refuse to recognize, through appropriate enforcement measures, the creditor's acquisition of title in pursuance of that statute. (*See* pp. 161-62, n. 11.)

Justice Stevens in his dissent adopted the correct "state action" analysis, recognizing that the constitutionality of section 7-210—"state action" if anything is—was the underlying issue in the case. Moreover, he appeared to adopt the Legalist model, distinguishing the state as lawmaker and thus bearer of Fourteenth Amendment duties from private actors like Flagg Brothers merely following the procedure laid down by state law. (*See* pp. 176-77.) Stevens failed, however, to discuss how section 1983 reached Flagg Brothers as defendant.

43. Cuyler v. Sullivan, 446 U.S. 335 (1980). In this case the Court stated that while the delicts of privately retained criminal defense attorneys are not attributable to the state, the state's action of securing a criminal conviction of one who is inadequately represented by counsel *is* subject to the Fourteenth Amendment. The case presents no problems for the Legalist model.

44. Parratt v. Taylor, 451 U.S. 527 (1981). This is one of the most important recent Supreme Court cases insofar as choice of models is concerned. The Court held that the negligent loss of a prisoner's personal property by prison officials, *for which loss an adequate remedy existed under state law,* did not constitute a denial of due process law. The case appears to reject the Governmental and Naturalist models in favor of the Legalist model, at least with respect to nondeliberate infliction of injury to constitutionally protected interests. *See also* Ingraham v. Wright, 430 U.S. 651 (1977); Alexander and Horton, *"Ingraham v. Wright:* A Primer for Cruel and Unusual Jurisprudence," 52 S. Cal. L. Rev. 1305, 1393-99 (1979).

Although the decision in *Parratt* is structurally consistent with the Legalist model, Justice Rehnquist's opinion for the Court in that case is not. In *Parratt,* Rehnquist in effect held that the Nebraska state remedies were adequate to remedy the constitutional violation represented by the officials' negligence. Such a holding flies in the face of the time-honored principle that state remedies for federal constitutional violations need not be exhausted before a section 1983 action may be brought in federal court. The Legalist would instead argue that the result in *Parratt* is correct if the act of official negligence in that case was not an act of lawmaking. If the negligent act was not lawmaking, it was not part of the state's legal regime and therefore could not be unconstitutional. The Legalist would then point out the constitutional adequacy of the state's legal regime, which itself provided a remedy for the injury suffered.

One confusing strand in Justice Rehnquist's opinion for the court is the emphasis on *procedural* due process. As Martin Redish correctly points out, the case really has nothing to do with procedural due process, since a worry with procedure assumes that the person with the loss is quarreling with the process that led up to it rather than with the loss itself. [*See* Redish, "Abstention, Separation of Powers, and the Limits of the Judicial Function," 94 Yale L.J. 71, 98-102 [1984]. *See also* Monaghan, "State Law Wrongs, State Law Remedies, and the Fourteenth Amendment," 86 Colum. L. Rev. 979, 984-86 [1986].) Redish also correctly identifies the sweeping implications of *Parratt* as a case endorsing what we call the Legalist model: Acts of state officers that are illegal and adequately remedied under state law would not be federally reviewable.

45. Polk County v. Dodson, 454 U.S. 312 (1981). This was a section 1983 suit brought by a criminal defendant against his court-appointed public defender in which the claim was inadequate representation resulting in a deprivation of due process. The public defender was paid by the county. Nevertheless, the Court held that her acts were not attributable to the state and hence not "state action" because her duty was to her client, not to the

state that paid her. She was not the "agent" of the state in her capacity as defense counsel.

The case is inconsistent with *Screws v. United States* [22], *Monroe v. Pape* [28], and other decisions that appear to adopt the Governmental model, as Justice Blackmun in dissent emphasized (pp. 328-34). Justice Powell, in his opinion for the Court, tried to distinguish those cases on the ground that in *Screws* and *Monroe* the delicts occurred during the exercise of power "possessed by virtue of state law and made possible only because the wrongdoer is clothed with the authority of state law" (pp. 317-18, quoting the line from United States v. Classic, 313 U.S. 299, 326 [1941], that was reiterated in *Screws* and *Monroe*). But the public defender's acts *were* such an exercise of state-granted power to exactly the same extent as the acts in *Screws* and *Monroe,* where the state granted the authority to arrest and to search but forbade beatings, illegal entries, and so forth. Moreover, the fact, stressed by Powell, that the public defender was the agent of the defendant does not entail that she was not simultaneously the agent of the state that paid her and directed her to represent indigents.

Polk County v. Dodson therefore sits uneasily with *Screws, Monroe,* and the other cases deeming illegal acts of state officials "state action" in the constitutional sense. When joined with *Parratt* [44] and *Hudson v. Palmer* [49], it strongly suggests repudiation of the governmental model.

46. Logan v. Zimmerman Brush Company, 455 U.S. 422 (1982). In this case, an Illinois remedy for employment discrimination was denied a discharged employee by a state commission and by the Illinois courts because the same state commission, through no fault of the employee, inadvertently failed to act on the employee's claim within the statutorily prescribed time limit. The Supreme Court held the denial of the remedy to be unconstitutional despite the alleged availability of a state tort remedy for compensation. The Court reconciled its decision with *Parratt* [44] by deeming the Illinois procedure itself to be unconstitutionally arbitrary and the tort remedy inadequate, although it divided over whether the arbitrariness was a deprivation of procedural due process or equal protection. (This division was predictable. *See* Alexander and Horton, "*Ingraham v. Wright:* A Primer for Cruel and Unusual Jurisprudence," 52 S. Cal. L. Rev. 1305, 1370-82 [1979].)

47. Rendell-Baker v. Kohn, 457 U.S. 830 (1982), and Blum v. Yaretsky, 457 U.S. 991 (1982). These cases both involved suits against private institutions for violation of constitutional rights. In *Rendell-Baker*, a private school receiving state funds fired several teachers without a hearing and allegedly because of opinions they voiced. In *Blum*, Medicaid patients at private nursing homes were discharged or transferred without notice or

hearings. In both cases the Court held for the private institution on the ground that it was not a state actor and thus could not violate the Fourteenth Amendment.

Of course, the Court was correct that the defendants in the suits were not state actors. On the Legalist model, that fact would rule out the possibility that *they* acted unconstitutionally. It would not rule out the possibility, however, that *the state,* by funding the defendants and then permitting them to discharge employees and patients without hearings and for opinions voiced, was acting unconstitutionally. (The Court dealt with the difficult precedent of *Burton v. Wilmington Parking Authority* [29] by merely declaring *Burton* to be inapposite.) Nor would it rule out the possibility that if the state were acting unconstitutionally, the proper constitutional remedy would be one imposed on the defendants, such as, for example, reinstatement of discharged employees or patients.

If the two cases support any model, it is surely the Legalist model. The Naturalist model is definitely impossible to square with the language of the opinions, if not the holdings themselves. (If the language is disregarded, the cases may actually have decided that the actions of *the state* in funding plus permitting the discharges were constitutional *on their merits*.)

48. Lugar v. Edmundson Oil Co., 457 U.S. 922 (1982). In *Lugar*, a debtor sued his creditor under section 1983 for attaching his property in accordance with an allegedly unconstitutional (for want of a pre-attachment hearing) state attachment law. The Court held that where there is state action, as there was in this case because a state official had issued a writ of attachment, a private actor can be deemed to be acting "under color of state law" for purposes of a section 1983 action.

Lugar is a terribly confused case. In the first place, it is hard to see why the issuance of the writ of attachment by the state official made the difference. Presumably the state's attachment procedures would not have been less constitutionally infirm had attachment been accomplished through some self-help measure, such as filing an affidavit with a court and then physically affixing a copy of it on the property in question. Therefore, in *Lugar*, what should have been essential was that there was an unconstitutional state law plus action by a private party in pursuance of it. But those elements were present in *Flagg Brothers* [42], which went the other way.

Second, the Court held that action "under color of state law" for purposes of section 1983 was identical to the "state action" requirement (p. 929). Yet, if one rejects the Naturalist model and the two Naturalist hybrids, one must conclude that the private creditor was not a state actor—that *Flagg Brothers* was correct on that score. Therefore, not being a state actor, the creditor would seem to be incapable of "state action," no matter how many state officials got involved. On the other hand, if the private creditor *were* a state actor, as the Naturalist model(s) suggest, the actions or inactions of the state officials would be irrelevant to the cause of action against the creditor.

Standing by itself, without reference to *Flagg Brothers, Lugar* appears to endorse the Legalist/Naturalist or Governmental/Naturalist models, if not the pure Naturalist model. Of course, even on the Legalist model, *Lugar* might be correctly decided, though not because *the creditor* acted unconstitutionally, but because the *remedy* for *the state's unconstitutional action* fell appropriately on the creditor who had benefited thereby.

49. Hudson v. Palmer, 468 U.S. 517 (1984). This decision extends the holding of *Parratt v. Taylor* [44], which involved *negligent* acts of state officials for which an adequate state remedy existed, to cases where state officials *intentionally* injure others or their property in violation of state law, and where adequate state remedies exist to redress the injuries. The Court implied throughout its opinion that acts of the state and acts of state officials in violation of state law were entirely separate categories. The case would, therefore, appear to be a resounding endorsement of the Legalist model and rejection of the Governmental model. Yet, *Monroe v. Pape* [28], *Screws v. United States* [22], et al., were nowhere mentioned. (*See* Monaghan, "State Law Wrongs, State Law Remedies, and the Fourteenth Amendment," 86 Colum. L. Rev. 979, 994-96 [1986].)

50. Oklahoma City v. Tuttle, 471 U.S. 808 (1985). This case implicitly supports the Legalist model and rejects the Governmental model and the two Governmental hybrid models. Plaintiff was the representative of the deceased victim of a police shooting and sued both the police officer who fired the fatal shots and the city that employed him under section 1983. The jury returned a verdict in favor of the officer, most likely on the ground that he has acted in good faith (p. 817 n.4); but it found the city to be liable due to inadequate training and supervision of its police officers.

The Supreme Court found the jury instructions improperly permitted the jury to infer the inadequacy of training and supervision from the single incident of the shooting and reversed the judgment for plaintiff. Nonetheless, the Court expressed no general objection to a jury's finding the laws such as those governing training of police to be unconstitutional but finding the acts of officials in pursuance of those laws to be "not unconstitutional." (The Court indeed surmised that the jury had found the officer's act to be "not unconstitutional" rather than, say, unconstitutional but immunized from liability. *See id.*) Under the Governmental hybrid models, such a possibility does not exist (though the remedial meta-regime may deem the officer to be immune from liability despite having acted unconstitutionally). *See also* City of Springfield v. Kibbe, 107 S. Ct. 1114 (1987).

51. Williamson County Regional Planning Commission v. Hamilton Bank, 473 U.S. 172 (1985). This case raises the interesting question within the Legalist model of when the process of making law is completed. The Court held that the administrative process for finally determining the permissibility of a land development project had not been completed, thus barring as unripe a federal challenge to the antidevelopment position of the local planning commission. The Court distinguished such cases as *McNeese v. Board of Education* and *Patsy v. Florida Board of Regents* [30] which rejected the need to exhaust state admistrative remedies before resorting to federal court, as having dealt with administrative review for legal error rather than administrative review as part of the process of deciding what the law shall be. *See also* Macdonald, et al. v. Yolo County, 106 S. Ct. 2561 (1986).

52. Daniels v. Williams, 106 S. Ct. 662 (1986), and Davidson v. Cannon, 106 S. Ct. 668 (1986). These companion cases, though confusing on many points, appear to move a step beyond *Parratt* [44] in the direction of the Legalist model. Daniels, a state prisoner, brought a section 1983 damages action in federal court against a jailer who allegedly negligently left a pillow on a jail stairway, causing Daniels to slip and suffer injuries. Davidson, also a state prisoner, brought a section 1983 damages action against prison officials for allegedly negligently failing to protect him from another inmate. Justice Rehnquist, writing for a five-justice majority, held that actions against state officials premised on their negligence do not state federal constitutional grievances under the due process clause and cannot be brought under section 1983.

The step in the direction of the Legalist model consisted in Rehnquist's rejection of *Parratt*'s dictum that negligence of government officials could amount to unconstitutional conduct under the due process clause. If the injurious conduct complained of in *Daniels* was clearly not lawmaking, and that complained of in *Davidson* was arguably not lawmaking, then on the Legalist model that conduct could not be unconstitutional.

From a Legalist standpoint, the problem with Rehnquist's opinions in *Daniels* and *Davidson* is his denial of the relevance of the state's immunizing the officials from tort liability. Tort immunities are part of a state's legal regime and subject to substantive constitutional assessment. While in *Daniels* it was unclear whether such immunity existed, in *Davidson* it concededly did; and Rehnquist denied its relevance in both cases (pp. 666, 670-71).

The Legalist would have examined fully the substantive constitutional merits of the state laws that failed to provide Daniels and Davidson with damages remedies against their jailors. (In *Davidson*, the Legalist, like the *Davidson* dissenters, would also ask whether the prison officials' deliberate failure to give Davidson additional protection was an unconstitutional bit of lawmaking [pp. 673-74].) The Legalist might conclude, as did Justice Stevens in his separate concurrence, that the failure to provide a tort remedy was not itself unconstitutional (pp. 680-81). There were tort remedies available against the attacking inmate in *Davidson*, albeit of little value; there was medical care available free in prison; and there was insurance available to plaintiffs in both cases. *See* Appendix B, which follows. The Legalist would not, however, conclude—as Rehnquist concluded—that the nonexistence of tort remedies was irrelevant to the constitutional complaint; nor, on the other hand, would the Legalist follow the *Davidson* dissenters and characterize the state's grant of official immunity as an attempt to immunize the officials' constitutional violation (p. 676). If the officials' conduct was not lawmaking, their conduct could not be unconstitutional on the Legalist model. Hence, the grant of immunity, while it itself might be unconstitutional, could not be characterized as the dissenters would characterize it.

There is, however, a way of looking at *Daniels* and *Davidson* that does not characterize the Rehnquist opinion as one adopting the Legalist model. For Rehnquist could be saying that, regardless of the model adopted, the acts of the officials in *Daniels* and *Davidson* were not unconstitutional because they did not demonstrate hostility or indifference to constitutional values. Mere negligence (meaning failure to advert to a risk that is present) may indicate only a constitutional tragedy, not a constitutional violation.

53. *Pembaur v. City of Cincinnati,* 106 S. Ct. 1292 (1986). The issue in this case was explicitly the issue of what constitutes "lawmaking." Under the Court's decision in Monell v. Department of Social Services, 436 U.S. 658 (1978), municipalities could be liable in damages in section 1983 suits only for actions taken by their agents "pursuant to official municipal policy" (id., at 691). The question in *Pembaur* was whether a search and seizure conducted by a county sheriff's department after receiving advice from the county prosecutor represented the official policy of the county. The discussion among Justice Brennan, writing for the Court, Justice White, concurring, and Justice Powell, dissenting, regarding the nature of governmental policymaking is the first real attempt to grapple with a central question within the Legalist model. Of course, because the issue was only the liability of the county under the *Monell* principle, not the liability of the governmental employees, the Court did not have to adopt the Legalist model itself.

54. San Francisco Arts & Athletics, Inc. v. United States Olympic Committee, 107 S.Ct. 2971 (1987). The Supreme Court held that neither chartering of the USOC by the government, nor governmental assistance in obtaining funding for the USOC, nor the public interest in the functions performed by the USOC rendered the USOC a state actor subject to the Fifth Amendment's due process clause. (Pp. 2985-87.) The Court refused to

consider, on grounds that it was raised for the first time after the petition for certiorari was filed, a contention based on *Shelley v. Kraemer* [24] that the district court's injunction against the petitioner was "state action" subject to the Fifth Amendment (p. 2987, note 30).

Like *Rendell-Baker v. Kohn* and *Blum v. Yaretsky* [47], *San Francisco Arts* is definitely inconsistent with the Naturalist models and strongly supportive of the Legalist model. But the Court's refusal to deal directly with the contention that the *government's* act of issuing an injunction was unconstitutional represents one more confusing episode in the Court's struggle with the state-action tar baby.

(TWO) THIRTEENTH AMENDMENT DECISIONS

55. Hodges v. United States, 203 U.S. 1 (1906). In this case the Court held that the Thirteenth Amendment did not give the federal government authority to prosecute a private conspiracy of whites to intimidate blacks into not taking jobs at a lumber mill. Justice Brewer argued "that it was not the intent of the Amendment to denounce every act done to an individual which was wrong if done to a free man and yet justified in a condition of slavery" (p. 19). In essence Justice Brewer was construing the amendment along the lines of the Legalist model. Justice Harlan in dissent argued for a Naturalist-model reading of the amendment, so that all private acts injuring blacks because of their race that would have been permissible during slavery would be violations of the amendment.

56. Jones v. Alfred H. Mayer Co., 392 U.S. 409 (1968). In this case the Court interpreted 42 United States Code section 1982 to reach private racial discrimination and then upheld its constitutionality as a proper exercise of Congress' power to enforce the Thirteenth Amendment. In so doing the Court expressly overruled *Hodges v. United States* [55] (pp. 441-43 n. 78). *See also* Runyon v. McCrary, 427 U.S. 160 (1976).

(ONE) COMMERCE CLAUSE DECISION

57. *In re* Debs, 158 U.S. 564 (1985). In this case a federal court enjoined organizers of a railroad workers' strike from interfering thereby with interstate rail service. The question was whether private acts that interfere unduly with interstate commerce could be treated in the same manner as state governmental acts and struck down by the courts acting without direct Congressional authorization. The Supreme Court held that the federal government's power to regulate interstate commerce includes the power to eliminate private as well as governmental obstructions to such commerce, and that that power may be exercised by the federal judiciary as well as by Congress.

If one views dormant commerce clause jurisprudence as "constitutional" in the ordinary sense, then *Debs* stands for construing the "negative implications" aspect of the clause—the aspect that directly invalidates obstructions, as opposed to the aspect that authorizes federal legislation— on the Naturalist model, that is, as speaking to private action in addition to governmental action. If, on the other hand, one views dormant commerce clause jurisprudence as more akin to "interpretation of silent statutes," so that dormant commerce clause decisions are not "constitutional" decisions in the ordinary sense, then *Debs* stands for the proposition that some of Congress' "silent statutes" proscribe private acts as well as governmental ones. Finally, *Debs* can be read as interpreting the commerce clause to authorize judicial legislation in addition to Congressional legislation.

PULLMAN ABSTENTION DECISIONS

58. Railroad Commission of Texas v. Pullman, 312 U.S. 496 (1941). The Texas Railroad Commission ordered that all sleeping cars on railroads in Texas be in the charge of a Pullman conductor and not in the charge of a porter. Conductors were white, porters were black, and the latter, along with the railroads, claimed the commission's order was unauthorized by Texas law and violative of the equal protection clause of the Constitution. The Supreme Court held that because resolution of the question of state law, if in favor of the railroads and porters, would make resolution of the federal constitutional claim unnecessary, and because the answer to the state law question was far from clear, the case should be sent to the state courts for resolution of the state law question before the federal courts should proceed with the constitutional issue.

The decision in *Pullman* obviously supports the Legalist model. Interestingly, *Home Telephone & Telegraph* [11], which would appear to be diametrically opposed to *Pullman*, was never even mentioned by the unanimous *Pullman* Court.

See also Chicago v. Fieldcrest Dairies, 316 U.S. 168 (1942); Meridian v. Southern Bell Telephone & Telegraph Company, 358 U.S. 639 (1959); Harrison v. N.A.A.C.P., 360 U.S. 167 (1959); Martin v. Creasy, 360 U.S. 219 (1959); Bellotti v. Baird, 428 U.S. 132 (1976).

59. Harman v. Forssenius, 380 U.S. 528 (1965). In this case, the Court held the *Pullman* doctrine to be inapplicable where the state law is clear and the only basis for remitting the case to the state courts is to afford them the chance to invalidate the law. *See also* McNeese v. Board of Education [30].

Another case in which the Court declined to apply the *Pullman* doctrine—Baggett v. Bullitt, 377 U.S. 360 (1964)—stands for the proposition that *Pullman* abstention is improper where the very uncertainty of meaning of the state law that would otherwise be the basis of abstention itself renders the state law violative of the federal Constitution. *See also* Zwickler v. Koota, 389 U.S. 241 (1967).

Obviously, *Harman* and *Baggett* are consistent with the Legalist model, since in both cases it was the law of the state that was violative of the Constitution.

60. Reetz v. Bozanich, 397 U.S. 82 (1970). In this case the *Pullman* doctrine was applied to a clear state law that was possibly in violation of an unclear state constitutional provision. The Court invoked the policy of avoiding unnecessary federal constitutional decisions in support of its decision. *See also* Meridian v. Southern Bell Telephone & Telegraph Co., 358 U.S. 639 (1959); Askew v. Hargrave, 401 U.S. 476 (1971). *Cf.* Wisconsin v. Constantineau, 400 U.S. 433 (1971) (no need to abstain where no state constitutional provision appears to invalidate the law; four justices dissented on the ground that it was in fact unclear whether the law violated the state constitution).

61. Examining Board of Engineers, Architects, and Surveyors v. Flores de Otero, 426 U.S. 572 (1976). The Court in this case, without mentioning *Reetz* [60], refused to order abstention where broad provisions of the Puerto Rico Constitution might have invalidated the law in question. The Court relied on *Wisconsin v. Constantineau* [60] as authority for its refusal to abstain, though in that case no particular provision of Wisconsin's Constitution was directly pertinent. *Flores de Otero*, therefore, appears to mark a change in the model of unconstitutional state action from that employed in *Reetz*.

62. Hawaii Housing Authority v. Midkiff, 467 U.S. 229 (1984). In this case the shift in models that occurred in *Flores de Otero* [61] hardened into a rule. Hawaii's Constitution, like the federal one, proscribes takings not for a "public use." The appropriation of property at issue in the case was being challenged on the "public use" ground, but the Supreme Court held abstention to be unnecessary despite the fact that a restrictive state constitutional meaning of "public use" would have invalidated the action on state law grounds and avoided the necessity of a federal constitutional decision.

In our manuscript, we brought the catalog of Appendix A to an end with the conclusion of the United States Supreme Court's October 1986 term. As this book proceeded through galleys and page proofs in the Spring of 1988, we were tempted to add to the catalog with such cases as *City of St. Louis v. Praprotnik,* 108 S.Ct. 915 (decided March 2, 1988). Chronological catalogs, however, must be brought to an end somewhere. For publisher as well as for reader convenience, we maintain our original October 1986 term cutoff. Our invitation to readers is to use our catalog in Appendix A as a baseline, to be supplemented however might be desired as years go by after our cutoff date.

Appendix B

The Models of the Constitution's Referent (and States of Mind of Government Officials) in "Constitutional Tort" Actions

The area of "torts" committed by government officials has proved to be particularly vexing to courts and commentators alike. In this appendix we shall examine the area from the perspectives of our models of the Constitution's referent and explain why the area proves so resistant to clear, straightforward constitutional analysis.

Although the relevant acts of officials vary considerably in detail, those that are particularly troublesome for our purposes have the following features in common:

1. The acts injure persons or their property.
2. The acts, by injuring persons or their property, or by risking such injury, implicate constitutional values (CVs).
3. The acts are not punished by fines or imprisonment.
4. The acts are usually neither expressly "authorized" nor expressly "prohibited"; and if they are expressly prohibited, they are prohibited in terms of features of the acts to which the actors are not adverting at the time they act.

Acts of government officials that fit this general description raise two basic constitutional questions: (1) Is some sort of compensatory remedy demanded by the Constitution (the CVs), and, if so, from whom? (2) Was the act itself unconstitutional?

These questions are quite distinct. An official's act may be a constitutional violation, but the Constitution may not require the official to compensate the victim. For instance, where the official acted in "good faith,'' or where the official's task requires immunity from liability even when premised upon "bad faith," some sort of official immunity (qualified or absolute) may be demanded by the relevant *CV*s despite the unconstitutionality of the official's act and the fact that plaintiff's injury implicates *CV*s.

Not only is it possible that the Constitution does not demand compensation from the official, despite the official's constitutional violation, but also it is possible that the Constitution demands no remedy from the public fisc.[1] Or, if the Constitution demands some remedy from the public fisc, it may not demand a tort damages remedy. For example, a prisoner whose property is injured by nonmalicious acts of officials may be deemed to have suffered this injury as a result of an "unconstitutional" act; but given the harm to *CV*s of a damages action against the officials or the state, the Constitution may remit him to private, first-party insurance. Another prisoner, who suffers bodily injury as a result of nonmalicious but "unconstitutional" acts of officials, may have a constitutionally compelled remedy, not in tort damages, but in free, state-provided medical care and rehabilitation services in prison.

Not only is it possible that no damages remedy is compelled by a particular, injury-causing unconstitutional act, but it is also possible that the Constitution compels a remedy for injuries that are *not* the result of unconstitutional acts. Of course, this may be frequently true for the Legalist, since she may decide that the Constitution demands that a state's legal regime provide damages remedies for all sorts of injury-causing acts, most of which acts are not acts of lawmaking and thus not themselves "unconstitutional," However it is also true for the Naturalist and Governmentalist who have more expansive views of what count as "unconstitutional acts." Even they would concede that governmental "takings" are acts that are not intrinsically unconstitutional although a "remedy" ("just compensation") is constitutionally compelled. Indeed, there is probably a large number of acts that, on all models, are "not unconstitutional if, but only if, compensation is provided."

We therefore must always ask, with respect to the acts of government officials that fit our general description: Does the Constitution demand that the state provide a compensatory remedy for those injured by these acts; and, if so, from whom?

If the Constitution does *not* demand such a remedy, then we need proceed no further to ask whether those acts were unconstitutional; for regardless how we answer the latter question, the plaintiff is entitled to no remedy. (We are assuming that the official acts in question are always *ad hoc* responses to particular concrete situations rather than the establishment of some policy to govern the future cases. If they are the latter, then, if the acts are or would be unconstitutional, an injunctive and/or declaratory remedy would be available.)

If the Constitution does demand a compensatory remedy for these acts, the next question is, does the state provide the constitutionally compelled remedy? If it *does not*, then the state's legal regime is unconstitutional; and on all models—Legalist, Naturalist, Governmental, and hybrids—the constitutionally compelled remedy is available through the remedial meta-regime in either state court or federal court (except where the remedy is against the public fisc and is relegated solely to state court by the Eleventh Amendment).

If the state does provide the constitutionally compelled remedy, the only remaining question is, was the official's act "unconstitutional"? How that question is answered will affect only the choice of court for pursuing the constitutionally compelled remedy.

If the act was *not unconstitutional*, the constitutionally compelled remedy can be sought only in state court; neither the state nor anyone else has violated the Constitution on any model. There is no basis for invoking the remedial meta-regime.[2] (The constitutionally compelled remedy is here part of the state's primary legal regime, not part of the remedial meta-regime; for that remedy is *not* a remedy for an unconstitutional act.)

If the official's act *was unconstitutional,* then the constitutionally compelled remedy, while provided by the state's legal regime, is also available in federal court under the remedial meta-regime. For the remedy *is* a response to an unconstitutional act.

Now it is at the point of assessing the unconstitutionality of the official's act that the Legalist's analysis diverges from the analysis of the Naturalist and Governmentalist.

The Legalist must determine both (1) whether the official's act was an act of lawmaking and, if so, (2) whether it was unconstitutional. If the Legalist decides the act was not one of lawmaking, she never reaches the question of constitutional merits. Or rather she must deem the act to be "not unconstitutional" regardless of its merits because for the Legalist only "laws" can be unconstitutional.

The Naturalist and Governmentalist, on the other hand, will proceed directly to the second question, having no need under their models to answer the first.

Now the Legalist's question—was the official's act an act of lawmaking?—is a conceptual question that relates to the scope of the Legalist model itself.

The type of official act with which we are dealing here is by hypothesis one that is not expressly authorized by some norm that is clearly a "law." If it were expressly authorized, the Legalist could focus on the constitutionality of the authorizing law and not worry about whether the act authorized is itself a "law." But although the type of official act in question is not expressly authorized, it is also either not expressly forbidden or, if expressly forbidden, is forbidden in terms of features to which the actor did not advert at the time of the act.

The question then for the Legalist is whether to include official acts that fit this description within the legal regime that is the Legalist model's focus. This question identifies a difficult and controversial conceptual issue, and we take no stand either on its resolution or on what policy considerations should guide the Legalist. For our purposes it is sufficient to point out that the issue is one of the boundary questions that the Legalist must answer in order to employ her model.[3] Indeed, it is perhaps more important *that* the Legalist answer the question than *how* the question is answered.

This boundary question surfaces to plague the Supreme Court whenever the Court appears to be employing the Legalist model in connection with injury-causing official acts.

For example, in *Pembaur v. City of Cincinnati* (1986),[4] the liability of the county defendant was dependent upon a Legalist analysis given prior decisions limiting governmental liability under section 1983 to injuries caused by "lawmaking." The Court could not come up with a cogent analysis of lawmaking and essentially transferred the problem to the lower courts.

And in *Davidson v. Cannon* (1986),[5] although the Court hinted that the official's acts fell short of "lawmaking," its discussion of this point was muddied by the Court's more clearly made point that no damages remedy was constitutionally compelled. The latter point was both arguably correct (given that a prisoner's bodily injuries are probably treated free of charge by the state, and that a prisoner has little in the way of lost earnings), and, if correct, mooted the issue of "lawmaking."

If the official's act is deemed by the Legalist to be "lawmaking," then the Legalist rejoins the Naturalist and Governmentalist for the final question: Was the act unconstitutional despite the existence of a state remedy?

The difficulty *that* question presents is this: (1) Viewed from the standpoint of the actual *CV*-relevant costs and benefits that the act entailed—the God's-eye standpoint of total omniscience—the act should not have been undertaken. (2) However, as the decisionmaker viewed the situation at the time of decision, the act represented a reasonable choice in light of the *CV*-relevant costs and benefits discounted by their perceived probabilities; and if the decisionmaker's view of the situation was itself "unreasonable," that view nonetheless was neither the product of past, unreasonable decisions nor the product of indifference or hostility to *CV*s.

The abstract analysis in this appendix can be illustrated by considering the recent case of *Davidson v. Cannon* (1986).[6]

Davidson, a prisoner, filed a section 1983 action in federal court against prison officials based on the following facts, as described by Justice Blackmun writing in dissent:[7]

Davidson broke up a fight between two other inmates. Two days later, on Friday, December 19, 1980, the three were brought before a prison disciplinary officer. Only one of the three, Gibbs, was found guilty of fighting. When Davidson and the other inmate, McMillian, returned to their unit, McMillian threatened Davidson. Davidson decided to report the threat, in part to exonerate himself in advance but primarily to get the prison officials to take precautions. . . . Accordingly, Davidson reported the threat to Officer Garcia. Because McMillian had a history of prison assaults and fighting, . . . Garcia recognized the seriousness of McMillian's threats. Garcia had Davidson relate the incident in writing. He then took Davidson's note, and told Davidson to return to his unit.

Garcia delivered the note to respondent Cannon, Assistant Superintendent of the prison, and described its contents. Cannon did not think the threat serious because Davidson had not personally come to him to report it and because of the nature of the earlier fight. . . . Cannon nonetheless asked to speak to Davidson, but changed his mind when he learned that Davidson had already returned to his unit. . . . Rather than take one of the usual preventive measures, such as separating the two inmates, placing Davidson in protective custody, or attempting to ascertain the gravity of the threat by talking to the two, . . . Cannon simply told Garcia to pass the note along to respondent James, a corrections sergeant in the Internal Affairs Unit. . . .

Garcia followed Cannon's order, giving the note to James at approximately 2:15 p.m., and informing James that it concerned a threat to Davidson by McMillian. . . . Because James was not ordered to act immediately, he decided there was no urgency. James also decided not to follow the normal procedure of interviewing the complainant. . . . James had two other tasks that he considered to be of higher priority, . . . paperwork and a report of a knife in a cell. James described the latter as an emergency situation; he conceded, however, that that cell had been double locked so that it was secure. . . . James' regular shift ended at 4 p.m., but he worked a second shift that night as Assistant Center Keeper until 10:30 p.m. The Center Keeper ordinarily investigates threats to inmates, but again James took no action on the threat to Davidson . . . . The second shift was "normal and routine." . . . James made at least two conscious decisions not to act on the note; by the time he left the prison, he had forgotten about it. . . . Had he remembered, he would

have notified the weekend shift. . . . A reported threat would not
normally be ignored over the weekend. . . .

   Meanwhile, the prison authorities had been alerted to the potential
violence through another channel. On Wednesday, December 17,
Officer Gibson wrote a "Special Report" stating that an inmate
source had told him the fight involving Davidson and McMillian was
"not over yet." Gibson recommended keeping Davidson and Gibbs in
the detention area for their own protection. . . . This recommenda-
tion was apparently ignored, as both Davidson and McMillian
remained in their regular unit.

   Neither Cannon nor James worked during the weekend. . . . On
Sunday, December 21, McMillian attacked Davidson, . . . inflicting
the injuries that gave rise to this suit.

Now the Legalist, Naturalist, and Governmentalist should all begin their
inquiries by examining those relevant norms that uncontroversially are part
of the state's legal regime: the laws specifically governing the training,
supervision, and conduct of prison officials; the laws sanctioning improper
conduct by those officials; and the laws providing remedies to those injured
by the officials' conduct. If any of those laws are improper, then on all
models Davidson should be entitled to bring an action, in either federal or
state court, premised upon the constitutionally based remedial meta-regime.
(The Court in *Davidson* did not discuss the constitutional adequacy of these
surrounding laws, except the laws governing compensation.)

   If the legal regime is otherwise constitutionally proper, and if the
compensation it offers—*which may be nothing*—is sufficient to meet
constitutional standards, then all that hangs on discovering a constitutional
violation on any of the models is the availability of the state-provided
remedy, if any, in federal court in addition to state court.

   The Court in *Davidson* held that the state-granted immunity for the
defendant officials was constitutionally proper. The Court did not discuss
whether a state-provided remedy was available against the state treasury,
since that remedy would not be available, *under section 1983 in federal
court,* even were a constitutional violation present and such a remedy the
preferred remedy under the remedial meta-regime.[8] The Court conceivably
believed that those state-provided remedies available to Davidson—a tort
action against McMillian (undoubtedly of little value); private, first-party
insurance; and the free state medical care and rehabilitation provided
prisoners—were constitutionally adequate. If so, a federal action premised
upon a constitutional violation would, even if successful, net Davidson no
more than what the state was already providing. And a suit against the
prison officials would be unavailing.

   If, contrary to the Court's holding, the Constitution requires a damages
remedy against the officials, then—whether or not the state provides one—a

federal suit for damages remains possible on all the models. The Legalist must then find that the officials' actions amounted to lawmaking, and that as lawmaking the actions were unconstitutional. The Naturalist and Governmentalist would proceed directly to the constitutionality of the officials' acts.

We have nothing further to say about the Legalist's definition of lawmaking. Our readers should ask themselves which, if any, of the actions taken by the officials meet their (the readers') criteria for "laws." Focusing now on the ultimate question regarding the acts' constitutional merits, a question common to all the models, the readers should consider the above narrative of the events in *Davidson* and ask which decisions in the chain of events that led to Davidson's injuries represented an improper concern for constitutional values. Did Garcia, Cannon, or James make any decision that an official who had proper regard for the Constitution would not make? Was James' forgetting about the threat to Davidson a constitutionally improper "decision," or was it merely the inevitable though regrettable consequence of prior, quite proper decisions?

Again, the problem at this stage is not whether the Constitution should compel that some kind of remedy against someone be provided Davidson. The problem here is how the notion of unconstitutional action should be unpacked in the context of specific acts that result in harm to constitutional values.

We believe we have explained why the "constitutional tort" cases are so difficult for the courts:

1. The cases raise the problem of how to assess the constitutionality of specific acts rather than general rules, when those acts can be described quite differently depending upon whether they are described from the objective standpoint of their actual effects or from the subjective standpoint of the actor at the time of action.

2. The cases raise, for the Legalist, the conceptual problem of defining "lawmaking" in the context of discrete official acts.

3. The cases raise the problem of defining constitutionally adequate state remedies.

4. And the cases raise the subtle and neglected point that where constitutionally adequate state remedies exist, the only consequence of finding a constitutional violation is the availability of federal remedies in lieu of the parallel state remedies.

Notes

1. INTRODUCTION

1. A word of explanation is in order for the use of the abstract concept of "constitutional value" rather than some concrete value such as freedom of expression or equal protection.

Our project in this book is to describe and analyze some very general models of the Constitution's relationship to lawmakers, to other government officials, and to private citizens. These models can be applied to numerous constitutional values and the constitutional provisions that express those values. Although the exemplary use of a particular constitutional value would provide the reader and us with the advantage of concrete illustrations of our points, it also would create a danger that to us at least more than offsets any advantage. The use of a particular constitutional value would invite the reader to quarrel with our substantive interpretation of that value and, in quarreling, perhaps to miss the points we are attempting to make.

The points we wish to make in this book do not hang on such substantive interpretations. Those points, including the point that they are independent of substantive issues, are subtle and difficult enough without the added distraction of irrelevant substantive quibbles. In any event, if the reader feels in need of adding flesh to "constitutional value"—or, as we have abstracted it still further, CV—she may find it useful to provide her own illustrations.

2. We also happily concede that some CVs may be strategic, instrumental values, the purpose of which is to effect the realization of some more ultimate value or values to the maximum extent possible. *See,* e.g., Sager, "Foreword: State Courts and the Strategic Space Between the Norms and Rules of Constitutional Law," 63 Tex. L. Rev. 959, 962-63 (1985). And, of course, some judicial doctrines might be best understood not as statements of what CVs demand in some ideal sense but rather as strategic norms that are justified as instrumental to the fullest possible realization of CVs in a nonideal world. *See* ibid.; Bevier, "The First Amendment and Political Speech: An Inquiry into the Substance and Limits of Principle," 30

Stan. L. Rev. 299, 325-31 (1978) (arguing for the strategic nature of certain First Amendment doctrines).

Indeed, one might distinguish among an indefinite number of normative levels, ranging from what would be morally ideal in the most ideal world conceivable, to what would be morally ideal in our world were it ideal, to what would be morally ideal in the concrete situations in which we find ourselves. The lines separating axiological, moral, political, and constitutional theory (and, within the last, the line separating constitutional ideals from constitutionally derived strategies for nonideal situations) are extremely elusive if not impossible to draw. *See* Wonnell, "Problems in the Application of Political Philosophy to Law," 86 Mich. L. Rev. 123 (1987). On the practical paradoxes created by these different normative levels, see Alexander, "Pursuing the Good—Indirectly," 95 Ethics 315 (1985).

3. It may be fair to say that only two modern commentators have even disentangled the question from other questions with which it is associated. But although Laurence Tribe and Henry Monaghan have recognized the question's existence and nature, their approaches to its answer have thus far been quite superficial. *See* L. Tribe, *Constitutional Choices* (Cambridge: Harvard Univ. Press, 1985); Monaghan, "State Law Wrongs, State Law Remedies, and the Fourteenth Amendment," 86 Columbia L. Rev. 979 (1986).

4. 334 U.S. 1 (1948). See Appendix A, no. 24.

5. 436 U.S. 149 (1978). See Appendix A, no. 42.

6. 457 U.S. 922 (1982). See Appendix A, no. 48.

7. 365 U.S. 167 (1961). See Appendix A, no. 28.

8. 451 U.S. 527 (1981). See Appendix A, no. 44.

9. 106 S. Ct. 1292 (1986). See Appendix A, no. 53.

10. 365 U.S. 167 (1961). See Appendix A, no. 28.

11. 455 U.S. 422 (1982). See Appendix A, no. 46.

12. 106 S. Ct. 668 (1986). See Appendix A, no. 52.

13. 397 U.S. 82 (1970). See Appendix A, no. 60.

14. 467 U.S. 229 (1984). See Appendix A, no. 62.

15. *See* note 1.

2. THE LEGALIST MODEL

1. Again note that many *individual* laws are "permitted" only on the assumption that they do not coexist with certain other laws, even laws that may otherwise be "permitted" themselves. In other words, most of the time we cannot say of an individual law that it is "permitted"; we can say this only of entire legal regimes.

2. Of course, some individual laws can render unconstitutional *any* legal regime of which they are a part. Examples might be overly vague criminal statutes or overbroad regulations of speech. (Even these examples make some assumptions about the remaining laws of the legal regime, e.g., that the remaining laws do not clarify the vague law or narrow the overbroad law.) Another example might be a law that is (otherwise) constitutionally permissible but not constitutionally mandated and that is enacted for improper motives, such as to express racial hostility.

The constitutionality of other laws cannot be evaluated out of context of the larger set of laws of which they are a part. For example, a state use tax on goods purchased out-of-state may be constitutional or unconstitutional depending upon whether the state has a comparable sales tax on goods purchased within the state. *See* Henneford v. Silas Mason Co., 300 U.S. 577 (1937).

3. Remedial laws are also important in an entirely different sense. Within the set of laws we call the Constitution there may be express or implied prescriptions concerning whether and how to remedy injuries to persons caused by the presence and application of unconstitutional (invalid) legal regimes. Thus the Constitution might prescribe relief, with respect to particular unconstitutional laws, against the public fisc, against public officials, and even against private persons.

But note, the Constitution's primary focus on the Legalist model is not constitutional injury to those who suffer it and demand relief, but rather the sets of nonconstitutional legal regimes (including those regimes' remedial laws) the Constitution governs. Remedial norms within the Constitution itself—what we will label as the "remedial meta-regime" (*See* Chapter 8, text accompanying notes 3-6)—are necessarily secondary to the notion of unconstitutional legal regimes, because it is harm caused by unconstitutional legal regimes (which legal regimes include nonconstitutional remedial laws) that is the predicate for application of those remedial norms.

4. *See* R. Dworkin, *Taking Rights Seriously* (Cambridge: Harvard Univ. Press, 1977) 81-130.

5. *See* H.L.A. Hart, *The Concept of Law* (Oxford: Oxford Univ. Press, 1961) 97-114.

6. At times the Supreme Court has treated as delegations of governmental (lawmaking) powers laws that in many respects looked very much like ordinary property laws. *See* e.g., Larkin v. Grendel's Den, Inc., 459 U.S. 116 (1982); Washington *ex rel.* Seattle Trust Co., v. Roberge, 278 U.S. 116 (1928); Cusack Co. v. Chicago, 242 U.S. 526 (1917); Eubank v. Richmond, 226 U.S. 137 (1912).

We must reemphasize that the issue here is not an issue of who should win a lawsuit on the merits. Rather, the issue goes to the *nature of the suit* (constitutional versus nonconstitutional) and the *available forums* (federal or state). In other words, whether or not the delegate's *act* is one of "lawmaking," the *delegation* is surely a law (that permits the delegated act). Therefore, if, under the Legalist model, one cannot say the delegate acted unconstitutionally (because her acts are not acts of "lawmaking"), one can still say the delegating law itself is unconstitutional. *See* Planned Parenthood of Central Missouri v. Danforth, 428 U.S. 52, 67-72 (1976).

(One apparent exception to our claim that the characterization of the delegation is irrelevant to the merits of a suit is when the constitutional issue concerns the limits of delegation of lawmaking power. The exception is apparent only, because the characterization of a delegated power as one of "lawmaking" where the issue is "excessive delegation" under constitutional doctrines relating to separation of powers need not track the characterization of that power where the issue is instead how to employ our models of to whom the Constitution speaks.)

One other point. To be precise, when we speak about private ordering as "lawmaking," we are really speaking about the translation of private persons' choices into legally sanctioned coercion of others. *See* Ellickson, "Cities and Homeowner Associations," 130 U. Pa. L. Rev. 1519, 1520 (1982).

7. 106 S. Ct. 1292 (1986). See Appendix A, no. 53.

8. The absence of a remedy-providing law also would not resolve the status of the administrator's decision, which might still fail whatever criteria the Legalist model

demands for counting for a "law." Of course, the absence of such a remedy might itself be an unconstitutional defect in the legal regime. If it were not—that is, if no remedy is constitutionally required for the administrator's decision—the status of that decision may be theoretically unclear but will be practically irrelevant. That is so, ex hypothesis, because even if it *is* an "unconstitutional law" on the Legalist model, no remedy would be constitutionally compelled.

9. *See* Citizens' St. R. v. City Ry., 56 Fed. 746, 752 (C.C.D. Ind. 1893); Barnett, "What Is 'State' Action Under the Fourteenth, Fifteenth, and Nineteenth Amendments of the Constitution?", 24 Ore. L. Rev. 227, 229 (1945).

The problem here is similar to the problem of unconstitutional overbreadth. Since the Constitution can be read into every law as a limit on its scope, how can any law be overbroad? *See* Alexander, "Is There an Overbreadth Doctrine?", 22 San Diego L. Rev. 541 (1985).

10. Of course, if officials ceased complying with the Constitution's mandates on a widespread basis, the Constitution might on most theories of legal positivism cease to be fundamental law; but so long as it is fundamental law, it is duty-imposing on lawmakers.

11. *Cf.* Monell v. Department of Social Services, 436 U.S. 658 (1978) (under 42 U.S.C.A. section 1983, local governmental bodies are not vicariously liable for acts of agents unless those acts are acts of "lawmaking").

12. Note again that no matter how these acts are characterized, as "lawmaking" versus as "illegal," the characterization does not affect whether a grievance is legally meritorious under *some* legal norm and whether the grievance is linked to a constitutional value; it affects only whether the grievance concerns a constitutional "violation," which may in turn affect the choice of forum and perhaps the choice of defendant.

13. The status of the citizen's "right to resist" illegal arrests by peace officers is quite controversial. *See* Lerblance, "Impending Unlawful Arrest: A Question of Authority and Criminal Liability," 61 Denver L. J. 655 (1984); Chevigny, "The Right to Resist an Unlawful Arrest," 78 Yale L. J. 1128 (1969); Note, "Defiance of Unlawful Authority," 83 Harv. L. Rev. 626 (1970); Special Project, "Self-Help: Extrajudicial Rights, Privileges and Remedies in Contemporary American Society," 37 Rutgers L. Rev. 845, 901-07 (1984).

It is possible to view the notion of an official act that is simultaneously both illegal and legally authorized, which the Supreme Court has employed in the area of sovereign immunity, as the catch-all concept of marginal acts of "lawmaking" on the Legalist model. The Court has employed this notion because the reigning doctrine in sovereign immunity cases requires that there be acts of officials that are neither legally unauthorized, nor authorized by unconstitutional laws, yet are still illegal. *See* Florida Department of State v. Treasure Salvors, Inc., 458 U.S. 670 (1982); Larson v. Domestic & Foreign Commerce Corp., 337 U.S. 682 (1949).

The idea of officials' acts that are "illegal yet legally authorized" has proved perplexing. *See* e.g., Pennhurst State School & Hosp. v. Halderman, 465 U.S. 89 (1984); Chemerinsky, "State Sovereignty and Federal Court Power: The Eleventh Amendment after *Pennhurst v. Halderman,*" 12 Hastings Const. L. Q. 643, 655-58 (1985); Currie, "Sovereign Immunity and Suits Against Government Officers," 1984 Sup. Ct. Rev. 149; Shapiro, "Wrong Turns: The Eleventh Amendment and the *Pennhurst* Case," 98 Harv. L. Rev. 61 (1984). Perhaps the key here is whether the official's illegal act, nonetheless carries presumptive authority so that the ordinary citizen cannot legally respond to the official's act as she can respond to other illegal acts, *See* e.g., Pembaur v. City of Cincinnati, 106 S. Ct. 1292 (1986), 1301-2 (White, J., concurring), 1308-10 (Powell, J., dissenting) (act of official may not represent policy of the government and yet still carry some finality), Appendix A, no. 53.

14. *See* Monroe v. Pape, 365 U.S. 167 (1961); Screws v. United States, 325 U.S. 91 (1945). See Appendix A, nos. 28 and 22.

15. Court orders must generally be obeyed until set aside, even if the orders are illegal. *See* Walker v. City of Birmingham, 388 U.S. 307 (1967); Note "Defiance of Unlawful Authority," 83 Harv. L. Rev. 626 (1970).

Of course, even ordinary citizens may "legally" temporarily deprive others of what the latter are legally entitled to in the following sense. If A legally owes B something, B may not use self-help but must resort to legal process to obtain her legal due. In that sense, A's "illegal" refusal to give B her due has a certain presumptive legal authority, much like an illegal court order. Yet if A's refusal counts as "lawmaking" on the Legalist model, the model is threatened with collapse into the other models. *See* Chapter 4, and text accompanying notes 10-15; Chapter 11, text accompanying notes 13 and 14.

16. *See* e.g., Parratt v. Taylor, 451 U.S. 527 (1981), Appendix Á, no. 44. *See* this chapter, text accompanying note 8; Appendix B.

17. *See* e.g., Pembaur v. City of cincinnati, 106 S. Ct. 1292 (1986): Davidson v. Cannon, 106 S. Ct. 668 (1986); Daniels v. Williams, 106 S. Ct. 662 (1986); Appendix A, nos. 52 and 53. *See* this chapter, text accompanying notes 7 and 8; Appendix B.

18. *See* Hawaii Housing Authority v. Midkiff, 467 U.S. 229 (1984); Examining Board of Engineers, Architects, and Surveyors v. Flores de Otero, 426 U.S. 572 (1976); Reetz v. Bozanich, 397 U.S. 82 (1970); Monroe v. Pape, 365 U.S. 167 (1961); Screws v. United States, 325 U.S. 91 (1945); Home Telephone & Telegraph Company v. City of Los Angeles, 227 U.S. 278 (1913); Barney v. City of New York, 193 U.S. 430 (1940); Appendix A, nos. 9, 11, 28, 60, 61, 62.

A closely related problem to that of "illegal laws" is the problem of when the process of lawmaking is complete. Recently the Supreme Court held that the "lawmaking" process with respect to administrative approval/disapproval of a land development project had not been completed at the time of federal challenge to the project's disapproval, and it remanded the challenger to the administrative process. Williamson County Regional Planning Com'n v. Hamilton Bank, 473 U.S. 172, 186-97 (1985); Appendix A, no. 51.

A more distantly related issue is raised by state constitutional provisions that are interpreted to have exactly the same content as federal constitutional provisions. *See* Michigan v. Long, 463 U.S. 1032 (1983); Redish, "Supreme Court Review of State Court 'Federal' Decisions: A Study in Interactive Federalism," 19 Ga. L. Rev. 861 (1985).

19. Why would anyone challenge an unenforced "law" as opposed to challenging the lack of its enforcement? (The latter challenge, unlike the former, presents no particular problem for the Legalist model.) The answer is that unenforced laws may have certain chilling effects, just like laws that violate the state's constitution and will not be enforced for that reason.

20. *See* G. Christie, *Law, Norms and Authority* (London: Duckworth, 1982) 7-27.

21. 365 U.S. 167 (1961). See Appendix A, no. 28.

22. 325 U.S. 91 (1945). See Appendix A, no. 22.

23. 451 U.S. 527 (1981) (existence of state tort remedy for negligent act of prison official precludes resort to federal court). See Appendix A, no. 44.

24. 468 U.S. 517 (1984) (*Parratt* principle applied to intentional tort of prison official). See Appendix A, no. 49. *See also* Note, "Unauthorized Conduct of State Officials Under the Fourteenth Amendment: *Hudson v. Palmer* and the Resurrection of Dead Doctrines," 85 Colum. L. Rev. 837 (1985).

25. 106 S. Ct. 662 (1986). See Appendix A, no. 52.

26. 106 S. Ct. 668 (1986). See Appendix A, no. 52.

27. 457 U.S. 922 (1982). See Appendix A, no. 48.

28. *See* e.g., this chapter, note 18.

29. *But see* this chapter, text accompanying note 18.

30. Pennhurst State School & Hosp. v. Halderman, 465 U.S. 89 (1984). *See generally* this chapter, note 13.

31. The "state action" decisions have been called a "conceptual disaster area." Black, "Foreword: State Action, Equal Protection, and California's Proposition 14," 81 Harv. L. Rev. 69, 95 (1967).

32. *See* Alexander, "Cutting the Gordian Knot: State Action and Self-Help Repossession," 2 Hastings Const. L. Q. 893 (1975); Barnett, "What Is 'State' Action Under the Fourteenth, Fifteenth, and Nineteenth Amendments of the Constitution?", 24 Ore. L. Rev. 227, 228-29 (1945); Brest, "State Action and Liberal Theory: A Casenote on *Flagg Brothers v. Brooks,* 130 U. Pa. L. Rev. 1296 (1982); Buchanan, "State Authorization, Class Discrimination, and the Fourteenth Amendment," 21 Houst. L. Rev. 1, 36-37 (1984); L. Tribe, *American Constitutional Law* (Mineola, N.Y.: Foundation Press, 1978) 1149-61. *See also* Van Alstyne and Karst, "State Action," 14 Stan. L. Rev. 3 (1961); Williams, "The Twilight of State Action," 41 Tex. L. Rev. 347 (1963). The general insight was first formalized by Jeremy Bentham. *See* H. Hart, *Essays on Bentham* (Oxford: Clarendon press, 1982) 112-18, 164-66.

3. THE NATURALIST MODEL

1. Of course, with respect to the Fourteenth Amendment in particular, as opposed to the Constitution generally, the Civil Rights Cases, 109 U.S. 3 (1883), are formidable precedent for rejecting the Naturalist model, though there are some more recent cases that appear to undermine that decision. *See,* e.g., Appendix A, nos. 6 and 33.

2. *See* R. Epstein, *Takings: Private Property and the Power of Eminent Domain* (Cambridge: Harvard Univ. Press, 1985) 35-36.

3. The Naturalist model is, of course, very difficult to square with the linguistic formulations of most constitutional provisions. For example, the Contracts Clause states: "No state shall . . . pass any . . . law. . . ." The Fourteenth Amendment forbids "any State [to] deprive any person of life, liberty, or property, without due process of law," and likewise forbids "any State . . . [to] deny . . . the equal protection of the laws." The Fifteenth Amendment explicitly makes the states its duty bearers. On the other hand, the Thirteenth Amendment presents no linguistic difficulties for the Naturalist. Nor do the Fourth Amendment's search and seizure clause, the Fifth Amendment's due process and takings clauses, or the Eighth

Amendment's cruel and unusual punishments proscription, U. S. Const., art. 1, sect. 10, para, 1; amend. 1; amend. 4; amend. 5; amend. 8; amend. 13; amend. 14; amend. 15.

4. *See* e.g., 28 U.S.C. sects. 1331, 1343.

5. *See,* e.g., 28 U.S.C. sects. 1331, 1332. *See also* Chapter 8, note 1.

4. THE GOVERNMENTAL MODEL

1. *See* Chapter 2, note 13, for related difficulties with the notion of "illegal but official" action.

2. *See* Chapter 2, note 14.

3. *See* Chapter 2, note 13.

4. *See,* e.g., Abernathy, "Expansion of the State Action Concept Under the Fourteenth Amendment," 43 Corn. L. Q. 375, 381-86 (1958).

5. Similar tests in the sovereign immunity area for identifying acts of officials that are illegal but neither unauthorized by law nor authorized by unconstitutional laws have proved to be unsatisfactory as well. *See* Chapter 2, note 13.

6. 325 U.S. 91, 111 (1945). *See* Appendix A, no. 22.

7. *Screws* has been criticized in the commentary. *See* Lewis, "The Meaning of State Action," 60 Colum. L. Rev. 1083, 1086-89 (1960). It has also been defended. *See* Abernathy, "Expansion of the State Action Concept Under the Fourteenth Amendment," 43 Corn. L. Q. 375, 381-86 (1958); Williams, "The Twilight of State Action," 41 Tex. L. Rev. 347, 354-55 (1963). *See also* Hale, "Unconstitutional Acts as Federal Crimes," 60 Harv. L. Rev. 65 (1946). An earlier article criticizing the case of Barney v. City of New York, 193 U.S. 430 (1904), the reasoning in which case the *Screws* Court rejected, and which article was cited approvingly by Justice Rutledge in *Screws*, was Isseks, "Jurisdiction of the Lower Federal Courts to Enjoin Unauthorized Action of State Officials," 40 Harv. L. Rev. 969 (1927).

8. The sovereign immunity cases have been faced with this incoherent notion. *See* Chapter 2, note 13. But so, too, have the "state action" cases. Compare Monroe v. Pape, 365 U.S. 167 (1961) and Screws v. United States, 325 U.S. 91 (1941) (illegal acts committed under color of law) with Polk County v. Dodson, 454 U.S. 312 (1981) (*contra*). See Appendix A, nos. 28, 22, and 45.

9. We suggest that whatever virtues some might perceive in the "pretense" and "agency" tests for making the Governmental model workable are probably better conceived of as suggestions for identifying features of official actions that make those actions "lawmaking" on the Legalist model. As we pointed out, an expanded Legalist model could count as "lawmaking" acts that are illegal yet carry some presumptive legal authority. *See* Chapter 2, text accompanying notes 11-19.

10. 227 U.S. 278 (1913). See Appendix A, no. 11.

11. Ibid., at 287.

12. And, of course, there are hybrids between the purely private citizen on the one hand and the government official on the other hand. Witness the independent contractor with government. *See* Note, "Section 1983 and the Independent Contractor," 74 Georgetown L. J. 457 (1985).

13. Of course, even if not legally entitled to a presumption of legality, the ordinance might carry the "pretense of authority"; but we have already discussed the inadequacies of the "pretense" test.

14. For example, the legal power of one wrongfully in possession to prevent self-

help by the rightful owner can be viewed as analogous to the legal power of some officials to have their illegal acts treated differently from ordinary illegal acts.

15. *See* Chapter 2, text accompanying notes 11-19.

16. This is, in fact, unlikely. The clause undoubtedly requires duty-imposing laws directed at private citizens—e.g., lynch mobs.

17. *See also* Tower v. Glover, 467 U.S. 914 (1984).

18. See the discussion in Chapter 9, note 24, of cases where government-employee status should be irrelevant to breach of constitutionally required norm. These cases demonstrate that the Naturalist model is a live option relative to the Governmental model. That is, not every provision (if any provision) speaks only to laws applicable only to government officials. Indeed, even the "cruel and unusual punishment" provision—our illustration in text—might apply to laws governing lynch mobs and independent contractors for punishment.

5. POSTSCRIPT TO THE NATURALIST AND GOVERNMENTAL MODELS: THE PROBLEM OF DEFINING "UNCONSTITUTIONAL ACTS"

1. The problem is not exclusive to "torts" as ordinarily understood. Note the debate over whether a contracting party ordinarily has a legal "right" to breach the contract so long as she is willing to pay damages, or instead has only a "power" to breach the contract. *See*, e.g., O. Holmes, Jr., *The Common Law* (Boston: Little, Brown and Company, 1881, 1963): 235-37. Of course, if one conceptualizes "torts" expansively—as including, for example, breaches of contract—then its boundaries are roughly coextensive with the boundaries of the problem of defining "unconstitutional acts" for purposes of our models.

2. If the state fails to provide a damages remedy, and the failure is not itself unconstitutional, the theoretical ambiguity concerning whether the act is "unconstitutional" may still remain, but it has no practical importance; the injured party would be entitled to no legal remedy from any court on any basis. If the state's failure to provide a damages remedy is itself unconstitutional, the theoretical ambiguity would again remain, and the failure to provide damages remedy would again have no practical significance; the injured party would be able to seek the constitutionally required remedy in federal court regardless of the model employed (Legalist or Naturalist) or the status of the injuring acts ("constitutional" or "unconstitutional"), because the *state* will have acted unconstitutionally on any model.

3. *See* Chapter 2, text accompanying notes 7-8. *See generally* Appendix B.

6. THREE HYBRID MODELS

1. 457 U.S. 922 (1982). *See* Appendix A, no. 48.

2. Regardless of which possibility—pure Naturalist or Legalist/Naturalist—is *the* possibility, *Lugar* is inconsistent with Flagg Brothers, Inc. v. Brooks, 436 U.S. 149 (1978), a structurally identical debtor-creditor section 1983 case, unless (implausibly) the warehousemen's law at issue in the latter was considered by the Court to be constitutional on its merits. *See* Appendix A, nos. 42 and 48. *See* Chapter 9, text accompanying notes 17-19.

3. *See generally* Appendix A.

4. It should be pointed out that the Legalist/Governmental hybrid model draws no support from the notion that the "state" acts only through its "agents." We have shown the agency argument to be problematic support for the pure Governmental model—because that model applies to officials acting in violation of constitutionally mandated laws and thus relies on the incoherent notion of "legally authorized illegal acts." *See* Chapter 4, text accompanying note 8.

On the other hand, as applied to the Legalist/Governmental hybrid model, the agency argument, though no longer faced with the incoherent notion of "legally authorized illegal acts" (since the hybrid model applies only to acts that are "legal," though under unconstitutional laws), must now face the problem of distinguishing governmental officials from private citizens in the context of legally authorized (legally permitted or legally mandated) acts. The legal duties and permissions applicable to persons on the governmental payroll (not acting as lawmakers) are no different in any material way from the legal duties and permissions applicable to private citizens. The state carries out its purposes through both groups.

If the Legalist/Governmental hybrid draws no support from the notion that "the state acts only through agents," then does the more extensive Legalist/Naturalist hybrid draw support from that notion? Could not all persons, private citizens and government officials alike, who act in obedience to (or as permitted by) unconstitutional laws be thought of as the means through which the state achieves its intended unconstitutional states of affairs? And if so, doesn't this fact indicate that all persons who act as prescribed or permitted by unconstitutional laws are themselves violating the Constitution, as the Legalist/Naturalist hybrid model contends?

We deny that any support can be derived for the Legalist/Naturalist hybrid model from the fact that the "state" acts only through agents. The argument from agency is really an argument about when *the principal*—the "state"—has violated a constitutional command; *it is not an argument that shows the agent herself has violated a constitutional command.* And it is stipulated that wherever the Legalist/Naturalist hybrid model diverges from the Legalist model, the "state" *qua* lawmakers has acted unconstitutionally.

The question of whether all persons who comply with a state's unconstitutional laws are thereby the state's agents really amounts to nothing more than the question of whether the violation of the Constitution consists in (1) enactment of unconstitutional laws plus compliance by citizens and officials (with resulting harm to a constitutional value), or consists instead in (2) enactment of unconstitutional laws (which leads to compliance by citizens and officials, with resulting harm to a constitutional value). *That* question—whether the agent's act is itself part of the violation of the Constitution by the principal (the "state") or is just a harmful consequence of that violation—has no practical implications for constitutional litigation that we can discern. In most cases, there will be both enactment *and* compliance, or at least enactment and threatened compliance.

Suppose we view the argument—that a citizen's obedience to an unconstitutional law makes the citizen into the agent of the state—as an argument to the effect that when one is acting as an agent of the state, one is the state. Or, put differently, the state is nothing more than its agents. On this view, the citizen-agent is not herself a violator of constitutional commands, as the Legalist/Naturalist hybrid model maintains.

Although the view just identified would support the Legalist/Naturalist hybrid model, that model, as we shall demonstrate, may not differ in terms of any practical implications from the pure Legalist model. That is so because, if we assume the choice of model does not affect real-world culpability, then *the pure Legalist model does not differ in terms of practical implications from either the pure Governmental model or pure Naturalist model whenever the lawmakers enacted unconstitutional laws.* See Chapter 8 and Chapter 10. And since it is *only* when the lawmakers have enacted unconstitutional laws that the Legalist hybrid models diverge from the pure Legalist model, the Legalist hybrid models may have the same practical implications as the Legalist model. *See* Chapter 10.

5. *See* this chapter, text accompanying note 1.

6. Suits alleging threatened or past harm stemming from officials' compliance with unconstitutional state laws (as opposed to municipal laws—*see* Monell v. Department of Social Services, 436 U.S. 658 [1978])—cannot ordinarily be brought against the state *qua* state because of the Eleventh Amendment. *See* Ex Parte Young, 209 U.S. 123 (1908); Edelman v. Jordan, 415 U.S. 651 (1974).

7. *See* Chapter 4.

8. CHOICE OF FORUM, REMEDY, AND DEFENDANT

1. We take no position on whether federal courts *must* be vested with jurisdiction to hear all constitutional claims. *See generally* Clinton. "A Mandatory View of Federal Court Jurisdiction: A Guided Quest for the Original Understanding of Article III," 132 U. Pa. L. Rev. 741 (1984); Redish, "Constitutional Limitations on Congressional Power to Control Federal Jurisdiction: A Reaction to Professor Sager," 77 Nw.U. L. Rev. 143 (1982); Sager, "The Supreme Court, 1980 Term—Foreword: Constitutional Limitations on Congress' Authority to Regulate the Jurisdiction of the Federal Courts," 95 Harv. L. Rev. 17 (1981).

2. *See* Fuentes v. Shevin, 407 U.S. 67 (1972).

3. *See also* Chapter 2, note 3.

4. *See* e.g., Bivens v. Six Unknown Named Agents, 403 U.S. 388 (1971); Davis v. Passman, 442 U.S. 228 (1979); Carlson v. Green, 446 U.S. 14 (1980); Mt. Healthy City School District Board of Education v. Doyle, 429 U.S. 274 (1977) (applicability of *Bivens* to unconstitutional acts by state and local governments); K. Davis, *Administrative Law Treatise,* 2nd ed., Vol. 5 (San Diego: K. C. Davis Pub. Co., 1984) 147-52 (same).

5. *See, e.g.,* 42 U.S.C. sect. 1983. *See also* Chappell v. Wallace, 462 U.S. 296 (1983); Bush v. Lucas, 462 U.S. 367 (1983). Federal statutes designed to remedy constitutional violations—to implement the remedial meta-regime—as well as state judicial or legislative enactments for that purpose, must be adequate to that task, or else the federal courts will supplant those remedies with their own. But the constitutional remedies provided by federal statute or by the states, if adequate, need not be identical to those the federal courts would impose. *See* Dellinger, "Of Rights and Remedies: The Constitution as a Sword," 85 Harv. L. Rev. 1532, 1547-49 (1972); Steinman, "Backing Off *Bivens* and the Ramifications of This Retreat for the Vindication of First Amendment Rights," 83 Mich. L. Rev. 269 (1984). Put differently, the remedial meta-regime for any particular constitutional value may consist of alternative remedies, a point to which we will recur from time to time.

Of course, uncertainty over what the relevant state laws actually prescribe—unless that very uncertainty renders the laws violative of the Constitution (*see*, e.g., City of Houston v. Hill, 107 S.Ct. 2502 [1987]; Baggett v. Bullitt, 377 U.S. 360 [1964]; Zwickler v. Koota, 389 U.S. 241 [1967])—might be grounds for federal court abstention. *See* Railroad Commission of Texas v. Pullman, 312 U.S. 496 (1941), Appendix A, no. 58. In addition, commencement of a state proceeding that affords an opportunity to redress adequately any constitutional grievance would be grounds for the type of federal court abstention mandated by the *Younger v. Harris* line of cases. *See* Younger v. Harris, 401 U.S. 37 (1971); Hicks v. Miranda, 422 U.S. 332 (1975); Moore v. Sims, 442 U.S. 415 (1979). In either event, if the state courts (1) do not interpret the state laws in a manner that negates any constitutional grievance and (2) do not apply the federal constitutional remedial meta-regime in the event that the state laws cannot be rendered constitutional by mere interpretation, the federal courts can then do so on review.

It is important for the possibility of suit in federal court on the Legalist model that the distinction be maintained between what the constitutional values in question require of a legal regime and what those same constitutional values require by way of remedy if the legal regime is defective (the remedial meta-regime). Both the required legal regime and the remedial meta-regime are derived from the same constitutional values. If a state were required to have only an adequate remedial meta-regime in order not to be in violation of the Constitution, there could never be an original Constitution-based suit in federal court involving a challenge to a defective state legal regime on the Legalist model. That is so because it would always be possible that the highest state court would apply the constitutionally required remedial meta-regime to remedy the state's defective legal regime. For original suits in federal court to be a possibility on the Legalist model, it must be sufficient to allege that a state does not have the required legal regime. The remedial meta-regime—the required regime for remedying constitutional violations—is the responsibility of both state courts and the federal government. *See* Steffel v. Thompson, 415 U.S. 452 (1974) (refusing to require *Younger v. Harris* abstention where no pending state proceeding).

This point has as its corollary the point that the law of the state must, on the Legalist model, be distinguishable from the rulings of the state courts on federal constitutional grounds, that is, the state courts' enforcement of the remedial meta-regime. In other words, federally constitutionally defective state law, even when deemed defective by state courts, is still state law. (*See* Chapter 2, text accompanying notes 9-10, where we discuss the problem of distinguishing unconstitutional "laws" from "other things.")

With respect to this point, note the distinction between cases like Parratt v. Taylor, 451 U.S. 527 (1981), and Hudson v. Palmer, 468 U.S. 517 (1984), in which *state remedies negated any constitutional violation*, and cases like Ingraham v. Wright, 430 U.S. 651 (1977), in which, on the theory of the constitutional violation that was argued, *state remedies* could at most *compensate for the constitutional violation* but could not negate it. *See* Appendix A, nos. 44 and 49; Alexander and Horton, "*Ingraham v. Wright:* A Primer for Cruel and Unusual Jurisprudence," 52 S.Cal. L. Rev. 1305, 1393-99 (1979). Of course, thousands of cases arise in *state* courts involving challenges to state laws on *federal* constitutional grounds.

6. "The judicial Power of the United States . . . shall extend to all

Cases . . . arising under this Constitution" U.S. Const., art. III, sect. 2, para. 1.

7. Depending upon how the unconstitutional laws on creditors' remedies originated, *LM* might be a state or local legislature, the state courts, or a state or local administrative agency or officer. Various constitutional values might dictate various degrees of immunity from suit for each type of *LM*. *See,* e.g., Tenney v. Brandhove, 341 U.S. 367 (1951) (absolute immunity for legislators); Pierson v. Ray, 386 U.S. 547 (1967), and Stump v. Sparkman, 435 U.S. 349 (1978) (absolute immunity for judges acting within their jurisdiction); Scheuer v. Rhodes, 416 U.S. 232 (1974), Wood v. Strickland, 420 U.S. 308 (1975), Imbler v. Pachtman, 424 U.S. 409 (1976), Butz v. Economou, 438 U.S. 478 (1978), Nixon v. Fitzgerald, 457 U.S. 731 (1982), Harlow v. Fitzgerald, 457 U.S. 800 (1982), and Mitchell v. Forsyth, 472 U.S. 511 (1985) (varying degrees of immunity for various types of administrative officials).

8. The Eleventh Amendment rules out most constitutional suits against the *state* treasury *in federal court.* (Theoretically, the state courts should be open to suits against the state treasury if the relevant constitutional values identify the state treasury as the appropriate source for the constitutional remedy. *See* Wolcher, "Sovereign Immunity and the Supremacy Clause: Damages Against States in Their Own Courts for Constitutional Violations," 69 Cal. L. Rev. 189 [1981]; Note, "Section 1983 in State Court: A Remedy for Unconstitutional State Taxation," 95 Yale L. J. 414 [1985]. *See also* Amar, "Of Sovereignty and Federalism," 96 Yale L. J. 1425, 1477 n. 211 [1987].)

9. *See* this chapter, text accompanying note 6.

10. 457 U.S. 922 (1982). See Appendix A, no. 48.

11. In a recent article Eric Zagrans argues that section 1983 applies to private persons as well as government officials and institutions, but only when the laws are unconstitutional by virtue of authorizing or permitting the behavior in question. Zagrans does *not* adopt the Legalist model and argue that officials' acts contrary to constitutionally proper laws cannot be unconstitutional; he argues only that such acts are not the subject of section 1983 and that *Monroe v. Pape* was mistaken on this score. Zagrans, "Under Color of" *What Law:* A Reconstructed Model of Section 1983 Liability," 71 Va. L. Rev. 499 (1985).

12. *See* Edelman v. Jordan, 415 U.S. 651 (1974).

13. *See* Wolcher, "Sovereign Immunity and the Supremacy Clause: Damages Against States in Their Own Courts for Constitutional Violations," 69 Cal. L. Rev. 189 (1981). *See also* Amar, "Of Sovereignty and Federalism," 96 Yale L. J. 1425, 1477 n. 211 (1987).

14. *Lugar* was in fact a suit for consequential damages rather than restitution.

15. 209 U.S. 123 (1908).

16. Cf. Zagrans, "Under Color of" *What* Law: A Reconstructed Model of Section 1983 Liability," 71 Va. L. Rev. 499, 562-64 (1985) (arguing for a similar but somewhat different theory of *Ex Parte Young*).

There is another theory offered to justify *Ex Parte Young* that merits comment. On that theory, which draws from cases preceding *Young,* the state official is being sued under the common law of the state to enjoin his "tortious" conduct. The official will respond that his conduct—enforcement of the constitutionally challenged law—is not tortious because it is legally authorized. The plaintiff will then respond to the official's response by arguing the unconstitutionality and hence invalidity of the law and its concomitant authorization of enforcement. If that argument succeeds, what is left is an ordinary suit to enjoin a tort under state law.

This theory is unsuccessful for two reasons. First, it is not clear that there is original federal jurisdiction where the federal issue arises only in anticipation of the contents of the defendant's answer to the complaint. *See* M. Redish, *Federal Jurisdiction* (Indianapolis: The Bobbs-Merrill Co., 1980) 72-77.

Second, the theory does not cover cases where the official's conduct would *not* amount to a common law tort in the absence of authorization by the law in question. For example, if the law is challenged, not on due process grounds, but on equal protection grounds—for example, it confers a constitutionally optional benefit on others but does not confer it on plaintiff—the success of such a challenge would not amount to a showing of tortious conduct toward anyone. (If one wants to argue that the general enforcement of a legal regime is "tortious" if that regime is constitutionally defective in any of its parts, one may do so; but then the plaintiff's suit in "tort" would not arise under the legal regime itself, which is what the theory in question requires, but under the Constitution.)

17. Bivens v. Six Unknown Named Agents, 403 U.S. 388 (1971).

9. "STATE ACTION" AND THE SUBSTANTIVE MERITS

1. *See* Chapter 2, note 31.

2. Alexander, "Cutting the Gordian Knot: State Action and Self-Help Repossession," 2 Hastings Const. L. Q. 893 (1975).

3. H. Hart, *Essays on Bentham* (Oxford: Clarendon Press, 1982) 112-18, 164-66.

4. Again, the choice of court may affect the choice of defendant/remedy where the Constitution permits alternative defendant/remedy packages. *See* Chapter 8, text accompanying notes 4-5.

5. *See* Chapter 2, note 32.

Not only is the question of whether permissive laws or only their mandatory complements represent "state action" irrelevant to the merits of any constitutional issue—since, except in a condition of anarchy, all permissive laws take place within a framework of mandatory laws—but also, for similar reasons, the "Is state inaction 'state action'?" question is irrelevant. Whether the failure to enact law L_2 is a separate "state action" from the enactment of L_1, or whether the state has only acted in enacting L_1 without L_2 ($L_1 - L_2$), is again irrelevant to constitutional doctrine: the enactment of $L_1 - L_2$ is surely "state action." *See* Alexander, "Cutting the Gordian Knot: State Action and Self-Help Repossessions," 2 Hastings Const. L.Q. 893, 897 n. 16 (1975).

We also believe nothing hangs on the question of whether the *enactment* of preexisting law—by legislation, judicial decision, etc.—is the relevant "state action" for purposes of constitutional theory, or whether, as legal realists might claim, only its judicial application in a particular case is "state action," at least not when we are dealing with application by the highest court in the jurisdiction. *See* Chapter 2, text accompanying notes 15-18.

6. In the article referred to in this chapter, note 2, Alexander also said that his classification of categories of state action (proprietary, mandatory, permissive, etc.) was not the same as Hohfeld's, though Hohfeld's categories might be relevant to the constitutional merits. Alexander, "Cutting the Gordian Knot: State Action and Self-

Help Repossession,'' 2 Hastings Const. L. Q. 893, 896 n. 16 (1975) (citing W. Hohfeld, *Fundamental Legal Conceptions as Applied to Judicial Reasoning* [New Haven: Yale Univ. Press, 1923]). (That is, whether the state has created in private persons a privilege, a right, or a power may be constitutionally significant, though all three legal statuses would represent state action.)

It should also be stated that nothing with respect to ''state action''— *viewed as relevant to the substantive merits of a constitutional claim*—hinges on the question of how much must the state enforce a law on the books in order for us to say that the law on the books really is the law of the state. The reason why nothing hinges on this with respect to state action (as merits) is that what the state *is* doing—enforcing law X with Y effort—is what must be analyzed under whatever normative principles the constitutional scheme embodies, not whether enforcing X with Y effort makes X a ''law.'' (There are, of course, some issues relevant to the application of the Legalist model that arise when the law on the books, including the law on the books regarding efforts of enforcement, is not followed in practice. *See* Chapter 2, text accompanying notes 11-19.)

7. 334 U.S. 1 (1948). See Appendix A, no. 24.

8. For a representative sampling of cases implicitly recognizing that judicial formulation of mandatory/permissive laws is ''state action,'' *see, e.g.,* New York Times v. Sullivan, 376 U.S. 254 (1964), and its progeny; Zacchini v. Scripps-Howard Broadcasting Co., 433 U.S. 562 (1977); Martinez v. California, 444 U.S. 277 (1980); and NAACP v. Claiborne Hardware Co., 458 U.S. 886 (1982).

9. 245 U.S. 60 (1917).

10. *See* Alexander, ''Cutting the Gordian Knot: State Action and Self-Help Repossession,'' 2 Hastings Const. L. Q. 893, 902-05 (1975).

11. *See* Alexander, ''Cutting the Gordian Knot: State Action and Self-Help Repossession,'' 2 Hastings Const. L. Q. 893, 899-906 (1975); Goodman, ''Professor Brest on State Action and Liberal Theory, and a Postscript to Professor Stone,'' 130 U. Pa. L. Rev. 1331, 1339-43 (1982); Horowitz, ''The Misleading Search for 'State Action' Under the Fourteenth Amendment'', 30 S. Cal. L. Rev. 208 (1957).

12. *See,* e.g., New York Times v. Sullivan, 376 U.S. 254 (1964).

13. The Supreme Court has recognized as much on a number of occasions. *See,* e.g., Duke Power Co. v. Carolina Environmental Study Group, 438 U.S. 59, 82-94 (1978) (upholding constitutionality of law limiting tort damages but acknowledging that the Constitution applies to government's definitions and adjustments of rights between private parties); Usery v. Turner Elkhorn Mining Co., 428 U.S. 1 (1976) (upholding constitutionality of law creating new private cause of action); Truax v. Corrigan, 257 U.S. 312 (1921) (invalidating, on due process grounds, law withdrawing employers' injunctive remedy against striking employees); Bronson v. Kinzie, 42 U.S. (1 How.) 311 (1843) (invalidating, on contracts clause grounds, state denial of foreclosure remedy in suit between private mortgagee and mortgagor). *See generally* Currie, ''Positive and Negative Constitutional Rights,'' 53 U. Chi. L. Rev. 864, 874-80 (1986).

14. *Cf.* Olsen, ''The Myth of State Intervention in the Family,'' 18 U. Michigan J. Law Reform 835, 836-37, 842 (1985) (footnotes omitted):

> The incoherence argument against nonintervention in the family parallels the legal realists' argument against laissez faire. Both laissez faire and nonintervention in the family are false ideals. As long as a state exists and enforces any laws at all, it makes

political choices. The state cannot be neutral or remain uninvolved, nor would anyone want the state to do so. The staunchest supporters of laissez faire always insisted that the state protect their property interests and that courts enforce contracts and adjudicate torts. They took this state action for granted and chose not to consider such protection a form of state intervention. Yet the so-called "free market" does not function except for such laws; the free market could not exist independently of the state. The enforcement of property, tort, and contract law requires constant political choices that may benefit one economic actor, usually at the expense of another. As Robert Hale pointed out more than a half century ago, these legal decisions "are bound to affect the distribution of income and the direction of economic activities." Any choice the courts make will affect the market, and there is seldom any meaningful way to label one choice intervention and the other laissez faire. When the state enforces any of these laws it must make political decisions that affect society.

Similarly, the staunchest opponents of state intervention in the family will insist that the state reinforce parents' authority over their children. Familiar examples of this reinforcement include state officials returning runaway children and courts ordering incorrigible children to obey their parents or face incarceration in juvenile facilities. These state actions are not only widely supported, they are generally not considered state intervention in the family. Another category of state policies is even less likely to be thought of as intervention. Supporters of nonintervention insist that the state protect families from third-party interference. Imagine their reaction if the state stood idly by while doctors performed non-emergency surgery without the knowledge or permission of a ten-year-old patient's parents, or if neighbors prepared to take the child on their vacation against the wishes of the parents, or if the child decided to go live with his fourth grade teacher. Once the state undertakes to prevent such third-party action, the state must make numerous policy choices, such as what human grouping constitutes a family and what happens if parents disagree. These choices are bound to affect the decisions people make about forming families, the distribution of power within the family, and the assignment of tasks and roles among family members. The state is responsible for the background rules that affect people's domestic behaviors. Because the state is deeply implicated in the formation and functioning of families, it is nonsense to talk about whether the state does or does not intervene in the family. Neither "intervention" nor "nonintervention" is an accurate description of any particular set of policies, and the terms obscure rather than clarify the policy choices that society makes.

. . . .

The incoherence argument goes further and I believe is more fundamental than the protective intervention argument. The protective intervention argument treats nonintervention as a fully possible but sometimes unwise choice; the incoherence argument questions the basic coherence of the concepts intervention and nonintervention. The state defines the family and sets roles within the family; it is meaningless to talk about intervention or nonintervention, because the state constantly defines and redefines the family and adjusts and readjusts family roles. Nonintervention is a false ideal because it has no coherent meaning.

For example, suppose a good-natured, intelligent sovereign were to ascend the throne with a commitment to end state intervention in the family. Rather than being obvious, the policies she should pursue would be hopelessly ambiguous. Is she intervening if she makes divorces difficult, or intervening if she makes them easy? Does it constitute intervention or nonintervention to grant divorce at all? If a child runs away from her parents to go live with her aunt, would nonintervention require the sovereign to grant or to deny the parents' request for legal assistance to reclaim their child? Because complete agreement on family roles does not exist, and because these roles undergo change over time, the state cannot be said simply to ratify pre-existing family roles. The state is continuously affecting the family by influencing the distribution of power among individuals.

15. 326 U.S. 501 (1946). See Appendix A, no. 23.

16. *See also* Terry v. Adams, 345 U.S. 461, 469 (1953) (state permission to private political club deemed to be unconstitutional state action); Chemerinsky, "Rethinking State Action," 80 Nw. U. L. Rev. 503, 522-23 (1986).

17. "Cutting the Gordian Knot: State Action and Self-Help Repossession," 2 Hastings Const. L. Q. 893, 912-13 (1975). Professors Rowe and Tribe are among those who concur with the proposition that self-help creditors' remedies are *less* likely to be constitutional than state-assisted creditors' remedies. *See* Rowe, "The Emerging Threshold Approach to State Action Determinations: Trying to Make Sense of *Flagg Brothers, Inc. v. Brooks,*" 69 Geo. L. J. 945 (1981); L. Tribe, *Constitutional Choices* (Cambridge: Harvard Univ. Press, 1985) 254.

18. *See* Fuentes v. Shevin, 407 U.S. 67 (1972); Lugar v. Edmundson Oil Co., 457 U.S. 922 (1982). See Appendix A, no. 48.

19. Flagg Brothers, Inc. v. Brooks, 436 U.S. 149 (1978). *See also* Adams v. Southern California First National Bank, 492 F.2d 324 (9th Cir. 1973), *cert. den.* 419 U.S. 1006 (1974). See Appendix A, no. 42.

20. *See* Sniadach v. Family Finance Corp., 395 U.S. 337 (1969).

21. *See* Flagg Bros., Inc. v. Brooks, 436 U.S. 149 (1978).

22. Our colleague, Maimon Schwarzschild, is attempting to develop such a theory. Schwarzschild, "Value Pluralism and the Constitution: In Defense of the State Action Doctrine" (forthcoming).

23. Timothy Terrell has fashioned a similar theory in the area of determining to which deprivations procedural due process attaches. Terrell, "'Property,' 'Due Process,' and the Distinction Between Definition and Theory in Legal Adjudication," 70 Georgetown L. J. 861 (1982).

24. We are skeptical that the only instance in which *CV*s are implicated by permissive laws are those in which the private party with the permission has a monopoly status. *See* e.g., this chapter, text accompanying notes 13-16. Although such instances may make up the lion's share of those in which permissive laws violate the Constitution, it is surely conceivable that other characteristics besides monopoly may affect the constitutionality of permissive laws. A general permission to everyone to commit battery, while admittedly an extreme example, does serve to illustrate that some nonmonopolistic permissions look constitutionally dubious. And of course the creditor-debtor laws that the Supreme Court struck down are examples of nonmonopolistic permissive laws that failed the Court's (admittedly controversial) constitutional calculus. *See* North Georgia Finishing, Inc., v. Di-Chem, Inc., 419 U.S. 601 (1975); Fuentes v. Shevin, 407 U.S. 67 (1972); Sniadach v. Family Finance Corp., 395 U.S. 337 (1969).

Moreover, occasionally permissions granted to government officials appear constitutionally dubious for reasons that have nothing to do with the government's monopoly status. A legal permission to the drivers of public school buses to drive in a manner that is dangerous to bystanders surely appears to us to be no different from a similar permission to drivers of private school buses. It is hard to envision a court's deeming the former permission to be beyond constitutional review. But if the former permission can be unconstitutional, it is not because the driver's employer, the government, is a monopolist; and the reasons that will render the former permission unconstitutional will almost assuredly render the latter permission unconstitutional as well.

Sometimes governmental employment—who pays the actor's salary and what type of legal authority he possesses beyond that of ordinary citizens—is a factor that is constitutionally significant, given whatever norms are properly read into the Constitution. Thus, the factors that distinguish "governmental officials" from "independent contractors" from "ordinary citizens" will sometimes, and perhaps often, be relevant to constitutionality. But often the fact of government employment will be insufficient to bear the weight of a constitutional distinction, as in the school bus driver case. (And, as the repossession cases illustrate, not all distinctions will cut the same way, in favor of "private-citizen immunity, state-official liability.")

25. Note that the Supreme Court has treated the laws governing defamation suits by private citizens as subject to constitutional analysis (*see,* e.g., Gertz v. Robert Welch, Inc., 418 U.S. 323 [1974]; and where the private citizens are deemed to be "public figures," it has treated the laws governing their defamation suits the same as the laws governing defamation suits by government officials for purposes of constitutional analysis. *See,* e.g., Curtis Publishing Co. v. Butts, 388 U.S. 130 (1967). Indeed, the laws governing defamation suits by minor public officials are treated by the Court similarly to the laws governing defamation suits by purely private plaintiffs rather than similarly to the laws governing other public officials and public figutes. *See* Rosenblatt v. Baer, 383 U.S. 75 (1966).

26. 109 U.S. 3 (1883). See Appendix A, no. 6.

27. Erwin Chemerinsky reads the *Civil Rights Cases* this way. *See* Chemerinsky, "Rethinking State Action," 80 Nw. U. L. Rev. 503, 515 (1986).

28. Erwin Chemerinsky, whose analysis of state action is otherwise completely consistent with ours, at times appears to assume, as we do not, that accepting this analysis will have far-reaching implications for the merits of constitutional lawsuits. *See,* e.g., ibid., at 525-26; Chemerinsky, "More Is Not Less: A Rejoinder to Professor Marshall," 80 Nw. U. L. Rev. 571, 572, 576 (1986). We believe that the analysis likely would affect the result in some cases—such as the self-help repossession cases (*see* this chapter, text accompanying note 17)—but its implications for the results in other cases likely would be quite modest, or perhaps nonexistent.

Chemerinsky has little to say about "state action" *qua* choice of models. Some of his statements do imply rejection of the Naturalist model. *See,* e.g., ibid., at 575 ("[C]ourts would have no basis for action under the Constitution to protect rights from private infringement if the state provided a sufficient remedy.") But he makes other statements that could be construed as Naturalist. *See,* e.g., Chemerinsky, "Rethinking State Action," 80 Nw. U. L. Rev. 503, 525 (1986) ("[U]ltimately all private actions must comply with the Constitution"). The better reading of Chemerinsky, we believe, is that he is not a Naturalist.

29. This point, that the choice of models does not affect the *merits* of a grievance, though it does affect such things as whether the grievance is labeled a violation of the Constitution as opposed to a violation of nonconstitutional law and whether the grievance may be vindicated by a federal court, can be most dramatically illustrated by considering the question raised earlier (Chapter 2, note 6) of whether decisions made by private property owners regarding the use of their property are acts of "lawmaking."

Suppose, for example, that a private property owner refuses, out of prejudice, to admit blacks onto his property, a refusal permitted by state law. We know from

Washington v. Davis, 426 U.S. 229 (1976), among other cases, that laws enacted because of racial prejudice are generally violative of the equal protection clause. Won't the characterization of the property owner's act—as "lawmaking" versus as "something else"—affect the merits of the claim by blacks that they have been denied equal protection under the Legalist model? And if so, then doesn't the fact that the various descriptions of the Legalist model's reach have different implications for the merits also mean that the choice among models has implications for the merits?

We concede that *if* various descriptions of the Legalist model's reach had implications for the merits, then it would follow that the choice among models would have such implications. We deny, however, that the choice within the Legalist model over whether the property owner's act of forbidding entry is one of "lawmaking" has any implications for the merits. For it is perfectly consistent with the likes of *Washington v. Davis* to deny that *lawmaking-qua-acts-of-prejudiced-property-owners* violates the equal protection clauses merely because it is motivated by prejudice. A state or local government's acts based on racial prejudice have a constitutionally material difference in quality from the racially prejudiced acts of property owners, even if we wish to characterize the latter's acts like those of the former as "lawmaking."

10. THE CHOICE AMONG MODELS: ITS IMPLICATIONS SUMMARIZED

1. 436 U.S. 149 (1978) (sale of bailed goods by bailor in pursuance of New York's statutory version of the Uniform Commercial Code does not violate due process because not traceable to "state action"). See Appendix A, no. 42.

2. *Lugar v. Edmundson Oil Company* may be such a decision. *See* Chapter 8, text accompanying notes 10-11 and note 11. *See* Appendix A, no. 48.

3. 325 U.S. 91 (1945). See Appendix A, no. 22.

4. 365 U.S. 167 (1961). See Appendix A, no. 28.

5. *See* Appendix A, Part D, nos. 60-62.

6. *See* Gildin, "The Standard of Culpability in Section 1983 and *Bivens* Actions: The Prima Facie Case, Qualified Immunity and the Constitution," 11 Hofstra L. Rev. 557 (1983); Wells and Eaton, "Substantive Due Process and the Scope of Constitutional Torts," 18 Ga. L. Rev. 201 (1984); Whitman, "Constitutional Torts," 79 Mich. L. Rev. 5 (1980); Note, "Civil Rights Suits Against State and Local Governmental Entities and Officials: Rights of Action, Immunities, and Federalism," 53 S. Cal. L. Rev. 945 (1980); "Developments in the Law—Section 1983 and Federalism," 90 Harv. L. Rev. 1133 (1977); Note, "*Parratt v. Taylor:* Don't Make a Federal Case Out of It," 63 B.U. L. Rev. 1187 (1983); Note, "A Theory of Negligence for Constitutional Torts," 92 Yale L. J. 683 (1983); Note, "Unauthorized Deprivations of Property Under Color of Law: A Critique of the Supreme Court's Due Process Analysis in *Parratt v. Taylor,* and a Proposed Alternative Analysis," 36 Rutgers L. Rev. 179 (1983).

11. POSTSCRIPT: DO DIFFERENT MODELS APPLY TO DIFFERENT CONSTITUTIONAL PROVISIONS?

1. *See,* e.g., U.S. Constitution, art. II, sects. 2 and 3.

2. *See* Jones v. Alfred H. Mayer Co., 392 U.S. 409 (1968), Appendix A, no. 56;

L. Tribe, *American Constitutional Law* (Mineola, N.Y.: Foundation Press, 1978) 1147 n. 1. *But see* Hodges v. United States, 203 U.S. 1 (1906), Appendix A, no. 55.

3. *See In re* Debs, 158 U.S. 564 (1895), Appendix A, no. 57.

4. *See* Jones v. Alfred H. Mayer Co., 392 U.S. 409 (1968). *But see* Hodges v. United States, 203 U.S. 1 (1906). See Appendix A, nos. 55 and 56.

5. "Neither slavery nor involuntary servitude . . . shall exist" U.S. Const., amend. XIII, sect. 1.

6. *See* Robertson v. Baldwin, 165 U.S. 275 (1897); Butler v. Perry, 240 U.S. 328 (1916); Selective Draft Law Cases, 245 U.S. 366 (1918).

7. "The Congress shall have Power . . . to regulate commerce . . . among the several states" U.S. Const., art. I, sect. 8, paras, 1 and 3.

8. *See* Pennsylvania v. Wheeling & Belmont Bridge Co., 54 U.S. (13 How.) 518 (1852).

9. *See* Pennsylvania v. Wheeling & Belmont Bridge Co., 59 U.S. (18 How.) 421 (1855); In re Rahrer, 140 U.S. 545 (1891); Prudential Insurance Co. v. Benjamin, 328 U.S. 408 (1946).

10. *See* Dowling, "Interstate Commerce and State Power—Revised Version," 1947 Colum. L.Rev. 547.

11. 158 U.S. 564 (1895). See Appendix A, no. 57.

12. "The right of the people to be secure . . . against unreasonable searches and seizures . . . shall not be violated." U.S. Const., amend. IV.

13. *See* Chapter 4, text accompanying notes 13-15.

14. *See* Chapter 2, last paragraph.

APPENDIX B

1. The issue here goes beyond that of Eleventh Amendment sovereign immunity, which applies only in federal courts. *See* Wolcher, "Sovereign Immunity and the Supremacy Clause: Damages Against States in Their Own Courts for Constitutional Violations," 69 Cal. L. Rev. 189 (1981). Note, "Section 1983 in State Court: A Remedy for Unconstitutional State Taxation," 95 Yale L. J. 414 (1985). The Eleventh Amendment can be viewed as the expression of a *CV* that entails a modification of the constitutional remedial meta-regime, but only when invoked in federal court. *But see* Amar, "Of Sovereignty and Federalism," 96 Yale L. J. 1425 (1987).

2. *See* Williamson County Regional Planning Commission v. Hamilton Bank, 473 U.S. 172, 195-96 n. 14 (1985), and Appendix A, no. 51; Monaghan, "State Law Wrongs, State Law Remedies, and the Fourteenth Amendment," 86 Colum. L. Rev. 979, 989-90 (1986).

3. We have pointed out other boundary questions in the textual discussion of the Legalist model—*see* Chapter 2, text accompanying notes 11-19—including the question of whether official acts that are expressly forbidden can be laws in some circumstances. *See* Chapter 2, text accompanying notes 13-18.

4. 106 S. Ct. 1292 (1986). See Appendix A, no. 53.

5. 106 S. Ct. 668 (1986). See Appendix A, no. 52.

6. Ibid.

7. Ibid., at 672.

8. Section 1983, which provides no damages remedies against states, is only a

partial instantiation of the remedial meta-regime; and *Bivens* actions (Bivens v. Six Unknown Named Agents, 403 U.S. 388 [1971]) against state treasuries are precluded from the *federal* courts by the present interpretation of the Eleventh Amendment.

Alphabetical List of Cases

United States v. Classic, 313 U.S. 299 (1941)
Corrigan v. Buckley, 271 U.S. 323 (1926)
United States v. Cruikshank, 92 U.S. 542 (1876)
Curtis Publishing Co. v. Butts, 388 U.S. 130 (1967)
Cusack Co. v. Chicago, 242 U.S. 526 (1917)
Cuyler v. Sullivan, 446 U.S. 335 (1980)
Damico v. California, 389 U.S. 416 (1967)
Daniels v. Williams, 106 S. Ct. 662 (1986)
Davidson v. Cannon, 106 S. Ct. 668 (1986)
Davis v. Passman, 442 U.S. 228 (1979)
In re Debs, 158 U.S. 564 (1895)
Dennis v. Sparks, 449 U.S. 24 (1980)
Duke Power Co. v. Carolina Environmental Study Group, 438 U.S. 59 (1978)
Edelman v. Jordan, 415 U.S. 651 (1974)
Estelle v. Gamble, 429 U.S. 97 (1976)
Eubank v. Richmond, 226 U.S. 137 (1912)
Evans v. Abney, 396 U.S. 435 (1970)
Evans v. Newton, 382 U.S. 296 (1966)
Examining Board of Engineers, Architects, and Surveyors v. Flores de Otero, 426
    U.S. 572 (1976)
Flagg Brothers Inc., v. Brooks, 436 U.S. 149 (1978)
Florida Department of State v. Treasure Salvors, Inc., 458 U.S. 670 (1982)
Fuentes v. Shevin, 407 U.S. 67 (1972)
Gertz v. Robert Welch, Inc., 418 U.S. 323 (1974)
Gibson v. Mississippi, 162 U.S. 565 (1896)
Gilmore v. City of Montgomery, 417 U.S. 556 (1974)
Gray v. Sanders, 372 U.S. 368 (1963)
Greene v. Louisville & Interurban Railroad Company, 244 U.S. 499 (1917)
Griffin v. Maryland, 378 U.S. 130 (1964)
Guinn v. United States, 238 U.S. 347 (1915)
Hague v. Committee for Industrial Organization, 307 U.S. 496 (1939)
Hamilton Gas, Light and Coke Co. v. Hamilton City, 146 U.S. 258 (1892)
Harlow v. Fitzgerald, 457 U.S. 800 (1982)
Harman v. Forssenius, 380 U.S. 528 (1965)
United States v. Harris, 1206 U.S. 629 (1883).
Harrison v. N.A.A.C.P., 360 U.S. 167 (1959)
Hawaii Housing Authority v. Midkiff, 467 U.S. 229 (1984)
Henneford v. Silas Mason Co., 300 U.S. 577 (1937)
Hicks v. Miranda, 422 U.S. 332 (1975)
Hodges v. United States, 203 U.S. 1 (1906)
Home Telephone & Telegraph Company v. City of Los Angeles, 227 U.S. 278 (1913)
City of Houston v. Hill, 107 S. Ct. 2502 (1987)
Hudgens v. N.L.R.B., 424 U.S. 507 (1976)
Hudson v. Palmer, 468 U.S. 517 (1984)
Hunter v. Erickson, 393 U.S. 385 (1969)
Imbler v. Pachtman, 424 U.S. 409 (1976)
Ingraham v. Wright, 430 U.S. 651 (1977)
Iowa-Des Moines National Bank v. Bennett, 284 U.S. 239 (1931)

In re Rahrer, 140 U.S. 545 (1891)
Railroad Commission of Texas v. Pullman, 312 U.S. 496 (1941)
United States v. Raines, 362 U.S. 17 (1960)
Raymond v. Chicago Union Traction Company, 207 U.S. 20 (1907)
Reetz v. Bozanich, 397 U.S. 82 (1970)
Reitman v. Mulkey, 387 U.S. 369 (1967).
Rendell-Baker v. Kohn, 457 U.S. 830 (1982)
Robertson v. Baldwin, 165 U.S. 275 (1897)
Rosenblatt v. Baer, 383 U.S. 75 (1966)
Runyon v. McCrary, 427 U.S. 160 (1976)
San Francisco Arts & Athletics, Inc., v. United States Olympic Committee, 107
    S. Ct. 2971 (1987)
Saunders v. Shaw, 244 U.S. 317 (1917)
Scheuer v. Rhodes, 416 U.S. 232 (1974)
Scott v. McNeal, 154 U.S. 34 (1894)
Screws v. United States, 325 U.S. 91 (1945)
Selective Draft Law Cases, 245 U.S. 366 (1918)
Shelley v. Kraemer, 334 U.S. 1 (1948)
Siler v. Louisville & Nashville R.R. Co., 213 U.S. 175 (1909)
Smith v. Allwright, 321 U.S. 649 (1944)
Sniadach v. Family Finance Corp., 395 U.S. 337 (1969)
Snowden v. Hughes, 321 U.S. 1 (1944)
City of Springfield v. Kibbe, 107 S. Ct. 1114 (1987)
Steffel v. Thompson, 415 U.S. 452 (1974)
Stump v. Sparkman, 435 U.S. 349 (1978)
Tenney v. Brandhove, 341 U.S. 367 (1951)
Terry v. Adams, 345 U.S. 461 (1953)
Tower v. Glover, 467 U.S. 914 (1984)
Truax v. Corrigan, 257 U.S. 312 (1921)
Turner v. Memphis, 369 U.S. 350 (1962)
United States v. Classic, 313 U.S. 299 (1941).
United States v. Guest, 383 U.S. 745 (1966)
United States v. Price, 383 U.S. 787 (1966)
United States v. Raines, 362 U.S. 17 (1960)
Usery v. Turner Elkhorn Mining Co., 428 U.S. 1 (1976)
Ex Parte Virginia, 100 U.S. 339 (1879)
Virginia v. Rives, 100 U.S. 313 (1879)
Walker v. City of Birmingham, 388 U.S. 307 (1967)
Washington v. Davis, 426 U.S. 229 (1976)
Washington ex rel. Seattle Trust Co. v. Roberge, 278 U.S. 116 (1928)
Whitley v. Albers, 106 S. Ct. 1078 (1986)
Williams v. United States, 341 U.S. 97 (1951)
Williamson County Regional Planning Com'n v. Hamilton Bank, 473 U.S. 172
    (1985)
Wisconsin v. Constantineau, 400 U.S. 433 (1971)
In re Wood, 140 U.S. 278 (1891)
Wood v. Strickland, 420 U.S. 308 (1975)
Yick Wo v. Hopkins, 118 U.S. 356 (1886)

Chronological List of Cases

Bronson v. Kinzie, 42 U.S. (1 How.) 311 (1843)
Pennsylvania v. Wheeling & Belmont Bridge Co., 54 U.S. (13 How.) 518 (1852)
Pennsylvania v. Wheeling & Belmont Bridge Co., 59 U.S. (18 How.) 421 (1855)
United States v. Cruikshank, 92 U.S. 542 (1876)
Virginia v. Rives, 100 U.S. 313 (1879)
Ex Parte Virginia, 100 U.S. 339 (1879)
Neal v. Delaware, 103 U.S. 370 (1880)
Bush v. Kentucky, 107 U.S. 110 (1882)
United States v. Harris, 106 U.S. 629 (1883)
Civil Rights Cases, 109 U.S. 3 (1883)
Arrowsmith v. Harmoning, 118 U.S. 194 (1885)
Yick Wo v. Hopkins, 118 U.S. 356 (1886)
In re Wood, 140 U.S. 278 (1891)
In re Rahrer, 140 U.S. 545 (1891)
Hamilton Gas, Light and Coke Co. v. Hamilton City, 146 U.S. 258 (1892)
Citizens' St. R. v. City Ry., 56 Fed. 746 (C.C.D. Ind. 1893)
Scott v. McNeal, 154 U.S. 34 (1894)
In re Debs, 158 U.S. 564 (1895).
Gibson v. Mississippi, 162 U.S. 565 (1896)
Robertson v. Baldwin, 165 U.S. 275 (1897)
Chicago, Burlington and Quincy Railroad Company v. Chicago, 166 U.S. 226 (1897)
The Japanese Immigrant Case, 189 U.S. 86 (1903)
Barney v. City of New York, 193 U.S. 430 (1904)
Hodges v. United States, 203 U.S. 1 (1906)
Raymond v. Chicago Union Traction Company, 207 U.S. 20 (1907)
Ex Parte Young, 209 U.S. 123 (1908)
Siler v. Louisville & Nashville R.R. Co., 213 U.S. 175 (1909)
Memphis v. Cumberland Telephone Co., 218 U.S. 624 (1910)

Baggett v. Bullitt, 377 U.S. 360 (1964)
Griffin v. Maryland, 378 U.S. 130 (1964)
Harman v. Forssenius, 380 U.S. 528 (1965)
Evans v. Newton, 382 U.S. 296 (1966)
Rosenblatt v. Baer, 383 U.S. 75 (1966)
United States v. Guest, 383 U.S. 745 (1966)
United States v. Price, 383 U.S. 787 (1966)
Pierson v. Ray, 386 U.S. 547 (1967)
Reitman v. Mulkey, 387 U.S. 369 (1967)
Curtis Publishing Co. v. Butts, 388 U.S. 130 (1967)
Walker v. City of Birmingham, 388 U.S. 307 (1967)
Zwickler v. Koota, 389 U.S. 241 (1967)
Damico v. California, 389 U.S. 416 (1967)
Amalgamated Food Employees Union v. Logan Valley Plaza, 391 U.S. 308 (1968)
Jones v. Alfred H. Mayer Co., 392 U.S. 409 (1968)
Hunter v. Erickson, 393 U.S. 385 (1969)
Sniadach v. Family Finance Corp., 395 U.S. 337 (1969)
Evans v. Abney, 396 U.S. 435 (1970)
Reetz v. Bozanich, 397 U.S. 82 (1970)
Adickes v. S. H. Kress & Company, 398 U.S. 144 (1970)
Wisconsin v. Constantineau, 400 U.S. 433 (1971)
Younger v. Harris, 401 U.S. 37 (1971)
Askew v. Hargrave, 401 U.S. 476 (1971)
Bivens v. Six Unknown Named Agents of Federal Bureau of Narcotics, 403 U.S.
    388 (1971)
Fuentes v. Shevin, 407 U.S. 67 (1972)
Moose Lodge No. 107 v. Irvis, 407 U.S. 163 (1972)
Central Hardware Company v. N.L.R.B., 407 U.S. 539 (1972)
Lloyd Corporation v. Tanner, 407 U.S. 551 (1972)
Norwood v. Harrison, 413 U.S. 455 (1973)
Adams v. Southern California First National Bank, 492 F.2d 324 (9th Cir. 1973)
Steffel v. Thompson, 415 U.S. 452 (1974)
Edelman v. Jordan, 415 U.S. 651 (1974)
Scheuer v. Rhodes, 416 U.S. 232 (1974)
Gilmore v. City of Montgomery, 417 U.S. 556 (1974)
Gertz v. Robert Welch, Inc., 418 U.S. 323 (1974)
Jackson v. Metropolitan Edison Company, 419 U.S. 345 (1974)
North Georgia Finishing, Inc., v. Di-Chem, Inc., 419 U.S. 601 (1975).
Wood v. Strickland, 420 U.S. 308 (1975)
Hicks v. Miranda, 422 U.S. 332 (1975)
O'Connor v. Donaldson, 422 U.S. 563 (1975)
Imbler v. Pachtman, 424 U.S. 409 (1976)
Hudgens v. N.L.R.B., 424 U.S. 507 (1976)
Washington v. Davis, 426 U.S. 229 (1976)
Examining Board of Engineers, Architects, and Surveyors v. Flores de Otero, 426
    U.S. 572 (1976)
Runyon v. McCrary, 427 U.S. 160 (1976)
Usery v. Turner Elkhorn Mining Co., 428 U.S. 1 (1976)
Planned Parenthood of Central Missouri v. Danforth, 428 U.S. 52 (1976)

Bellotti v. Baird, 428 U.S. 132 (1976)
Estelle v. Gamble, 429 U.S. 97 (1976)
Mt. Healthy City School District Board of Education v. Doyle, 429 U.S. 274 (1977)
Ingraham v. Wright, 430 U.S. 651 (1977)
Zacchini v. Scripps-Howard Broadcasting Co., 433 U.S. 562 (1977)
Stump v. Sparkman, 435 U.S. 349 (1978)
Flagg Brothers Inc., v. Brooks, 436 U.S. 149 (1978)
Monell v. Department of Social Services, 436 U.S. 658 (1978)
Duke Power Co. v. Carolina Environmental Study Group, 438 U.S. 59 (1978)
Butz v. Economou, 438 U.S. 478 (1978)
Davis v. Passman, 442 U.S. 228 (1979)
Moore v. Sims, 442 U.S. 415 (1979)
Martinez v. California, 444 U.S. 277 (1980)
Carlson v. Green, 446 U.S. 14 (1980)
Cuyler v. Sullivan, 446 U.S. 335 (1980)
Dennis v. Sparks, 449 U.S. 24 (1980)
Parratt v. Taylor, 451 U.S. 527 (1981)
Polk County v. Dodson, 454 U.S. 312 (1981).
Logan v. Zimmerman Brush Company, 455 U.S. 422 (1982)
Patsy v. Florida Board of Regents, 457 U.S. 496 (1982)
Nixon v. Fitzgerald, 457 U.S. 731 (1982)
Harlow v. Fitzgerald, 457 U.S. 800 (1982)
Rendell-Baker v. Kohn, 457 U.S. 830 (1982)
Lugar v. Edmundson Oil Company, 457 U.S. 922 (1982)
Blum v. Yaretsky, 457 U.S. 991 (1982)
Florida Department of State v. Treasure Salvors, Inc., 458 U.S. 670 (1982)
NAACP v. Claiborne Hardware Co., 458 U.S. 886 (1982)
Larkin v. Grendel's Den, Inc., 459 U.S. 116 (1982)
Chappell v. Wallace, 462 U.S. 296 (1983)
Bush v. Lucas, 462 U.S. 367 (1983)
Michigan v. Long, 463 U.S. 1032 (1983)
Pennhurst State School & Hosp. v. Halderman, 465 U.S. 89 (1984)
Hawaii Housing Authority v. Midkiff, 467 U.S. 229 (1984)
Tower v. Glover, 467 U.S. 914 (1984)
Hudson v. Palmer, 468 U.S. 517 (1984)
Oklahoma City v. Tuttle, 471 U.S. 808 (1985)
Mitchell v. Forsyth, 472 U.S. 511 (1985)
Williamson County Regional Planning Com'n v. Hamilton Bank, 473 U.S. 172
    (1985)
Daniels v. Williams, 106 S. Ct. 662 (1986)
Davidson v. Cannon, 106 S. Ct. 668 (1986)
Whitley v. Albers, 106 S. Ct. 1078 (1986)
Pembaur v. City of Cincinnati, 106 S. Ct. 1292 (1986)
MacDonald, et al. v. Yolo County, 106 S. Ct. 2561 (1986)
City of Springfield v. Kibbe, 107 S. Ct. 1114 (1987)
City of Houston v. Hill, 107 S. Ct. 2502 (1987)
San Francisco Arts & Athletics, Inc. v. United States Olympic Committee, 107
    S. Ct. 2971 (1987)

Bibliography

ALPHABETICAL

Abernathy, "Expansion of the State Action Concept Under the Fourteenth Amendment," 43 Corn. L. Q. 375 (1958).

Alexander, "Cutting the Gordian Knot: State Action and Self-Help Repossession," 2 Hastings Const. L. Q. 893 (1975).

Alexander, "Is There an Overbreadth Doctrine?", 22 San Diego L. Rev. 541 (1985).

Alexander, "Pursuing the Good—Indirectly," 95 Ethics 315 (1985).

Alexander and Horton, "*Ingraham v. Wright:* A Primer for Cruel and Unusual Jurisprudence," 52 S. Cal. L. Rev. 1305 (1979).

Amar, "Of Sovereignty and Federalism," 96 Yale L. J. 1425 (1987).

Barnett, "What Is 'State' Action Under the Fourteenth, Fifteenth, and Nineteenth Amendments of the Constitution?" 24 Ore. L. Rev. 227 (1945).

Bevier, "The First Amendment and Political Speech: An Inquiry into the Substance and Limits of Principle," 30 Stanford L. Rev. 299 (1978).

Black, "Foreword: State Action, Equal Protection, and California's Proposition 14," 81 Harv. L. Rev. 69 (1967).

Brest, "State Action and Liberal Theory: A Casenote on *Flagg Brothers v. Brooks*, 130 U. Pa. L. Rev. 1296 (1982).

Buchanan, "State Authorization, Class Discrimination, and the Fourteenth Amendment," 21 Houst. L. Rev. 1 (1984).

Chemerinsky, "More Is Not Less: A Rejoinder to Professor Marshall," 80 Nw. U. L. Rev. 571 (1986).

Chemerinsky, "Rethinking State Action," 80 Nw. U. L. Rev. 503 (1986).

Chemerinsky, "State Sovereignty and Federal Court Power: The Eleventh Amendment after *Pennhurst v. Halderman*, 12 Hastings Const. L. Q. 643 (1985).

Chevigny, "The Right to Resist an Unlawful Arrest," 78 Yale L. J. 1128 (1969).

Christie, *Law, Norms and Authority* (London: Duckworth, 1982).

Note, "Civil Rights Suits Against State and Local Governmental Entities and

Officials: Rights of Action, Immunities, and Federalism," 53 S. Cal. L. Rev. 945 (1980).

Clinton, "A Mandatory View of Federal Court Jurisdiction: A Guided Quest for the Original Understanding of Article III," 132 U. Pa. L. Rev. 741 (1984).

Currie, "Positive and Negative Constitutional Rights," 53 U. Chi. L. Rev. 864 (1986).

Currie, "Sovereign Immunity and Suits Against Government Officers," 1984 Sup. Ct. Rev. 149.

Davis, *Administrative Law Treatise,* 2nd ed., Vol. 5 (San Diego: K. C. Davis Pub. Co., 1984).

Note, "Defiance of Unlawful Authority," 83 Harv. L. Rev. 626 (1970).

Dellinger, "Of Rights and Remedies: The Constitution as a Sword," 85 Harv. L. Rev. 1532 (1972).

Dowling, "Interstate Commerce and State Power—Revised Version," 1947 Colum. L. Rev. 547.

Dworkin, *Taking Rights Seriously* (Cambridge: Harvard Press, 1977).

Ellickson, "Cities and Homeowner Associations," 130 U. Pa. L. Rev. 1519 (1982).

Epstein, *Takings: Private Property and the Power of Eminent Domain* (Cambridge: Harvard Univ. Press, 1985).

Gildin, "The Standard of Culpability in Section 1983 and *Bivens* Actions: The Prima Facie Case, Qualified Immunity and the Constitution," 11 Hofstra L. Rev. 557 (1983).

Goodman, "Professor Brest on State Action and Liberal Theory, and a Postscript to Professor Stone," 130 U. Pa. L. Rev. 1331 (1982).

Hale, "Unconstitutional Acts as Federal Crimes," 60 Harv. L. Rev. 65 (1946).

Hart, *The Concept of Law* (Oxford: Oxford Univ. Press, 1961).

Hart, *Essays on Bentham* (Oxford: Clarendon Press, 1982).

Hohfeld, *Fundamental Legal Conceptions as Applied to Judicial Reasoning* (New Haven: Yale Univ. Press, 1923).

Holmes, Jr., *The Common Law* (Boston: Little, Brown and Company, 1881, 1963).

Horowitz, "The Misleading Search for 'State Action' Under the Fourteenth Amendment," 30 So. Cal. L. Rev. 208 (1957).

Isseks, "Jurisdiction of the Lower Federal Courts to Enjoin Unauthorized Action of State Officials," 40 Harv. L. Rev. 969 (1927).

Lerblance, "Impending Unlawful Arrest: A Question of Authority and Criminal Liability," 61 Denver L. J. 655 (1984).

Lewis, "The Meaning of State Action," 60 Colum. L. Rev. 1083 (1960).

Monaghan, "State Law Wrongs, State Law Remedies, and the Fourteenth Amendment," 86 Colum. L. Rev. 979 (1986).

Olsen, "The Myth of State Intervention in the Family," 18 U. Michigan J. Law Reform 835 (1985).

Note, "*Parratt v. Taylor*: Don't Make a Federal Case Out of It," 63 B. U. L. Rev. 1187 (1983).

Redish, "Abstention, Separation of Powers, and the Limits of the Judicial Function," 94 Yale L. J. 71 (1984).

Redish, "Constitutional Limitations on Congressional Power to Control Federal Jurisdictions: A Reaction to Professor Sager," 77 Nw. U. L. Rev. 143 (1982).

Redish, *Federal Jurisdiction* (Indianapolis: The Bobbs-Merrill Co., 1980).

Redish, "Supreme Court Review of State Court 'Federal' Decisions: A Study in Interactive Federalism," 19 Ga. L. Rev. 861 (1985).

Rowe, "The Emerging Threshold Approach to State Action Determinations: Trying to Make Sense of *Flagg Brothers, Inc. v. Brooks,*" 69 Geo. L. J. 945 (1981).

Sager, "Foreword: State Courts and the Strategic Space Between the Norms and Rules of Constitutional Law," 63 Tex. L. R. 959 (1985).

Sager, "The Supreme Court, 1980 Term—Foreword: Constitutional Limitations on Congress' Authority to Regulate the Jurisdiction of the Federal Courts," 95 Harv. L. Rev. 17 (1981).

Schwarzschild, "Value Pluralism and the Constitution: A Defence of the State Action Doctrine" (unpublished).

"Developments in the Law-Section 1983 and Federalism." 90 Harv. L. Rev. 1133 (1977).

Note, "Section 1983 and the Independent Contractor," 74 Georgetown L.J. 457 (1985).

Note, "Section 1983 in State Court: A Remedy for Unconstitutional State Taxation," 95 Yale L. J. 414 (1985).

Special Project, "Self-Help: Extrajudicial Rights, Privileges and Remedies in Contemporary American Society," 37 Rutgers L. Rev. 845 (1984).

Shapiro, "Wrong Turns: The Eleventh Amendment and the *Pennhurst* Case," 98 Harv. L. Rev. 61 (1984).

Steinman, "Backing Off *Bivens* and the Ramifications of This Retreat for the Vindication of First Amendment Rights," 83 Mich. L. Rev. 269 (1984).

Terrell, "'Property,' 'Due Process,' and the Distinction Between Definition and Theory in Legal Adjudication," 70 Georgetown L. J. 861 (1982).

Tribe, *American Constitutional Law* (Mineola, N.Y.: Foundation Press, 1978).

Tribe, *Constitutional Choices* (Cambridge: Harvard Univ. Press, 1985).

Note, "A Theory of Negligence for Constitutional Torts," 92 Yale L. J. 683 (1983).

Note, "Unauthorized Conduct of State Officials Under the Fourteenth Amendment: *Hudson v. Palmer* and the Resurrection of Dead Doctrines," 85 Colum. L. Rev. 837 (1985).

Note, "Unauthorized Deprivations of Property Under Color of Law: A Critique of the Supreme Court's Due Process Analysis in *Parratt v. Taylor*, and a Proposed Alternative Analysis," 36 Rutgers L. Rev. 179 (1983).

Van Alstyne and Karst, "State Action," 14 Stan. L. Rev. 3 (1961).

Wells and Eaton, "Substantive Due Process and the Scope of Constitutional Torts," 18 Ga. L. Rev. 201 (1984).

Whitman, "Constitutional Torts," 79 Mich. L. Rev. 5 (1980).

Williams, "The Twilight of State Action," 41 Tex. L. Rev. 347 (1963).

Wolcher, "Sovereign Immunity and the Supremacy Clause: Damages Against States in Their Own Courts for Constitutional Violations," 69 Cal. L. Rev. 189 (1981).

Wonnell, "Problems in the Application of Political Philosophy to Law," 86 Mich. L. Rev. 123 (1987).

Zagrans, "'Under Color of' *What* Law: A Reconstructed Model of Section 1983 Liability," 71 Va. L. Rev. 499 (1985).

CHRONOLOGICAL

Holmes, Jr., *The Common Law* (Boston: Little, Brown and Company, 1881, 1963).

Hohfeld, *Fundamental Legal Conceptions as Applied to Judicial Reasoning* (New Haven: Yale Univ. Press, 1923).

Isseks, "Jurisdiction of the Lower Federal Courts to Enjoin Unauthorized Action of State Officials," 40 Harv. L. Rev. 969 (1927).

Barnett, "What Is 'State' Action Under the Fourteenth, Fifteenth, and Nineteenth Amendments of the Constitution?" 24 Ore. L. Rev. 227 (1945).

Hale, "Unconstitutional Acts as Federal Crimes," 60 Harv. L. Rev. 65 (1946).

Dowling, "Interstate Commerce and State Power—Revised Version," 1947 Colum. L. Rev. 547.

Horowitz, "The Misleading Search for 'State Action' Under the Fourteenth Amendment," 30 So. Cal. L. Rev. 208 (1957).

Abernathy, "Expansion of the State Action Concept Under the Fourteenth Amendment," 43 Corn. L. Q. 375 (1958).

Lewis, "The Meaning of State Action," 60 Colum. L. Rev. 1083 (1960).

Hart, *The Concept of Law* (Oxford: Oxford Univ. Press, 1961).

Van Alstyne and Karst, "State Action," 14 Stan. L. Rev. 3 (1961).

Williams, "The Twilight of State Action," 41 Tex. L. Rev. 347 (1963).

Black, "Foreword: State Action, Equal Protection, and California's Proposition 14," 81 Harv. L. Rev. 69 (1967).

Chevigny, "The Right to Resist an Unlawful Arrest," 78 Yale L. J. 1128 (1969).

Note, "Defiance of Unlawful Authority," 83 Harv. L. Rev. 626 (1970).

Dellinger, "Of Rights and Remedies: The Constitution as a Sword," 85 Harv. L. Rev. 1532 (1972).

Alexander, "Cutting the Gordian Knot: State Action and Self-Help Repossession," 2 Hastings Const. L. Q. 893 (1975).

"Developments in the Law—Section 1983 and Federalism," 90 Harv. L. Rev. 1133 (1977).

Dworkin, *Taking Rights Seriously* (Cambridge: Harvard Press, 1977).

Bevier, "The First Amendment and Political Speech: An Inquiry into the Substance and Limits of Principle," 30 Stanford L. Rev. 299 (1978).

Tribe, *American Constitutional Law* (Mineola, N.Y.: Foundation Press, 1978).

Alexander and Horton, *"Ingraham v. Wright:* A Primer for Cruel and Unusual Jurisprudence," 52 S. Cal. L. Rev. 1305 (1979).

Note, "Civil Rights Suits Against State and Local Governmental Entities and Officials: Rights of Action, Immunities, and Federalism," 53 S. Cal. L. Rev. 945 (1980).

Redish, *Federal Jurisdiction* (Indianapolis: The Bobbs-Merrill Co., 1980).

Whitman, "Constitutional Torts," 79 Mich. L. Rev. 5 (1980).

Rowe, "The Emerging Threshold Approach to State Action Determinations: Trying to Make Sense of *Flagg Brothers, Inc. v. Brooks,*" 69 Geo. L. J. 945 (1981).

Sager, "The Supreme Court, 1980 Term—Foreword: Constitutional Limitations on Congress' Authority to Regulate the Jurisdiction of the Federal Courts," 95 Harv. L. Rev. 17 (1981).

Wolcher, "Sovereign Immunity and the Supremacy Clause: Damages Against

States in Their Own Courts for Constitutional Violations,'' 69 Cal. L. Rev. 189 (1981).

Brest, "State Action and Liberal Theory: A Casenote on *Flagg Brothers v. Brooks,* 130 U. Pa. L. Rev. 1296 (1982).

Christie, *Law, Norms and Authority* (London: Duckworth, 1982).

Ellickson, "Cities and Homeowner Associations," 130 U. Pa. L. Rev. 1519 (1982).

Goodman, "Professor Brest on State Action and Liberal Theory, and a Postscript to Professor Stone," 130 U. Pa. L. Rev. 1331 (1982).

Hart, *Essays on Bentham* (Oxford: Clarendon Press, 1982).

Redish, "Constitutional Limitations on Congressional Power to Control Federal Jurisdictions: A Reaction to Professor Sager," 77 Nw. U. L. Rev. 143 (1982).

Terrell, "'Property,' 'Due Process,' and the Distinction Between Definition and Theory in Legal Adjudication," 70 Georgetown L.J. 861 (1982).

Gildin, "The Standard of Culpability in Section 1983 and *Bivens* Actions: The Prima Facie Case, Qualified Immunity and the Constitution," 11 Hofstra L. Rev. 557 (1938).

Note, *"Parratt v. Taylor:* Don't Make a Federal Case Out of It," 63 B. U. L. Rev. 1187 (1983).

Note, 'A Theory of Negligence for Constitutional Torts," 92 Yale L. J. 683 (1983).

Note, "Unauthorized Deprivations of Property Under Color of Law: A Critique of the Supreme Court's Due Process Analysis in *Parratt v. Taylor,* and a Proposed Alternative Analysis," 36 Rutgers L. Rev. 179 (1983).

Buchanan, "State Authorization, Class Discrimination, and the Fourteenth Amendment," 21 Houst. L. Rev. 1 (1984).

Clinton, "A Mandatory View of Federal Court Jurisdiction: A Guided Quest for the Original Understanding of Article III," 132 U. Pa. L. Rev. 741 (1984).

Currie, "Sovereign Immunity and Suits Against Government Officers," 1984 Sup. Ct. Rev. 149.

Davis, *Administrative Law Treatise,* 2nd ed., Vol. 5 (San Diego: K. C. Davis Pub. Co., 1984).

Lerblance, "Impending Unlawful Arrest: A Question of Authority and Criminal Liability," 61 Denver L. J. 655 (1984).

Redish, "Abstention, Separation of Powers, and the Limits of the Judicial Function," 94 Yale L. J. 71 (1984).

Shapiro, "Wrong Turns: The Eleventh Amendment and the *Pennhurst* Case," 98 Harv. L. Rev. 61 (1984).

Special Project, "Self-Help: Extrajudicial Rights, Privileges and Remedies in Contemporary American Society," 37 Rutgers L. Rev. 845 (1984).

Steinman, "Backing Off *Bivens* and the Ramifications of This Retreat for the Vindication of First Amendment Rights," 83 Mich. L. Rev. 269 (1984).

Wells and Eaton, "Substantive Due Process and the Scope of Constitutional Torts," 18 Ga. L. Rev. 201 (1984).

Alexander, "Is There an Overbreadth Doctrine?" 22 San Diego L. Rev. 541 (1985).

Alexander, "Pursuing the Good—Indirectly," 95 Ethics 315 (1985).

Chemerinsky, "State Sovereignty and Federal Court Power: The Eleventh

Amendment after *Pennhurst v. Halderman*," 12 Hastings Const. L. Q. 643 (1985).

Epstein, *Takings: Private Property and the Power of Eminent Domain* (Cambridge: Harvard Univ. Press. 1985).

Note, "Unauthorized Conduct of State Officials Under the Fourteenth Amendment: *Hudson v. Palmer* and the Resurrection of Dead Doctrines," 85 Colum. L. Rev. 837 (1985).

Note, "Section 1983 and the Independent Contractor," 74 Georgetown L. J. 457 (1985).

Note, "Section 1983 in State Court: A Remedy for Unconstitutional State Taxation," 95 Yale L. J. 414 (1985).

Olsen, "The Myth of State Intervention in the Family," 18 U. Michigan J. Law Reform 835 (1985).

Redish, "Supreme Court Review of State Court 'Federal' Decisions: A Study in Interactive Federalism," 19 Ga. L. Rev. 861 (1985).

Sager, "Foreword: State Courts and the Strategic Space Between the Norms and Rules of Constitutional Law," 63 Tex. L. R. 959 (1985).

Tribe, *Constitutional Choices* (Cambridge: Harvard Univ. Press, 1985).

Zagrans, "'Under Color of' *What* Law: A Reconstructed Model of Section 1983 Liability," 71 Va. L. Rev. 499 (1985).

Chemerinsky, "More Is Not Less: A Rejoinder to Professor Marshall," 80 Nw. U. L. Rev. 571 (1986).

Chemerinsky, "Rethinking State Action," 80 Nw. U. L. Rev. 503 (1986).

Currie, "Positive and Negative Constitutional Rights," 53 U. Chi. L. Rev. 864 (1986).

Monaghan, "State Law Wrongs, State Law Remedies, and the Fourteenth Amendment," 86 Colum. L. Rev. 979 (1986).

Amar, "Of Sovereignty and Federalism," 96 Yale L. J. 1425 (1987).

Wonnell, "Problems in the Application of Political Philosophy to Law" 86 Mich. L. Dev. 123 (1987).

Schwarzschild, "Value Pluralism and the Constitution: A Defense of the State Action Doctrine" (unpublished).

Index

ABOUT THE AUTHORS

LARRY ALEXANDER is Professor of Law at the University of San Diego, where he has taught for eighteen years. He is a graduate of Williams College and Yale Law School. He has published extensively in legal and philosophical journals on constitutional law, jurisprudence, and moral theory.

PAUL HORTON is Professor of Law at the University of San Diego, where he has taught for thirteen years. He is a graduate of Occidental College, the Law Center of the University of Southern California (Juris Doctor), and Yale Law School (Masters of Law). His areas of publication include family law, securities litigation, constitutional law, and legal philosophy.